TYPES OF MUSICAL FORM
AND COMPOSITION

50 Ready-to-Use Activities
for Grades 3–9

TYPES OF MUSICAL FORM AND COMPOSITION

50 Ready-to-Use Activities for Grades 3–9

Audrey J. Adair

Illustrated by Leah Solsrud

MUSIC CURRICULUM ACTIVITIES LIBRARY

PARKER PUBLISHING COMPANY
West Nyack, New York 10994

Library of Congress Cataloging-in-Publication Data

Adair, Audrey J.
    Types of musical form nd composition.
    ISBN 0-13-934985-5
    (Music curriculum activities library ; unit 3)
    1. School music—Instruction and study.   2. Musical
form.   2. Music appreciation.   I. Title.   II. Series:
Adair, Audrey J.,   Music curriculum activities
library ; unit 3.
    MT10.A14   1987   unit 3
    372.8′7 s   87-8835
    [372.8′74]

Printed in the United States of America

10   9   8   7   6   5

ISBN 0-13-934985-5

ATTENTION: CORPORATIONS AND SCHOOLS

Parker Publishing Company books are available at quantity discounts with bulk
purchase for educational, business, or sales promotional use. For information,
please write to: Prentice Hall Special Sales, 240 Frisch Court, Paramus, NJ
07652. Please supply: title of book, ISBN number, quantity, how the book will be
used, date needed.

PARKER PUBLISHING COMPANY
West Nyack, NY 10994

A Simon & Schuster Company

On the World Wide Web at http://www.phdirect.com

Prentice-Hall International (UK) Limited, *London*
Prentice-Hall of Australia Pty. Limited, *Sydney*
Prentice-Hall Canada Inc., *Toronto*
Prentice-Hall Hispanoamericana, S.A., *Mexico*
Prentice-Hall of India Private Limited, *New Delhi*
Prentice-Hall of Japan, Inc., *Tokyo*
Simon & Schuster Asia Pte. Ltd., *Singapore*
Editora Prentice-Hall do Brasil, Ltda., *Rio de Janeiro*

About the Author

Audrey J. Adair has taught music at all levels in the Houston, Texas, and Dade County, Florida, public schools. She has served as a music consultant, music specialist, general music instructor, choir director, and classroom teacher. In addition, she has written a series of musical programs for assemblies and holiday events, conducted music workshops, organized music programs for the community, established glee club organizations, and done specialization work with gifted and special needs students. Currently, she directs and coordinates children's choirs, performs as soloist with flute as well as voice, and composes sacred music.

Mrs. Adair received her B.A. in Music Education from St. Olaf College in Northfield, Minnesota, and has done graduate work at the University of Houston and Florida Atlantic University in Fort Lauderdale. She is also the author of *Ready-to-Use Music Activities Kit* (Parker Publishing Company), a resource containing over 200 reproducible worksheets to teach basic music skills and concepts.

About the *Library*

The *Music Curriculum Activities Library* was developed for you, the busy classroom teacher or music specialist, to provide a variety of interesting, well-rounded, step-by-step activities ready for use in your music classroom. The *Library*'s seven carefully planned Units combine imagination, motivation, and student involvement to make learning as exciting as going on a field trip and as easy as listening to music.

The units of the *Music Curriculum Activities Library* are designed to be used separately or in conjunction with each other. Each Unit contains 50 *all new* ready-to-use music activity sheets that can be reproduced as many times as needed for use by individual students. These 350 illustrated, easy-to-read activities will turn even your most reluctant students into eager learners. Each Unit offers a wealth of information on the following topics:

Unit 1: *Basic Music Theory* develops an understanding of the basic elements of melody, rhythm, harmony, and dynamics.

Unit 2: *Reading and Writing Music* provides a source of reinforcement and instills confidence in the beginner performer through a wide range of note-reading and writing activities in the treble clef, bass clef, and in the clef of one's own instrument.

Unit 3: *Types of Musical Form and Composition* gives the student the foundation needed to enjoy worthwhile music by becoming acquainted with a wide variety of styles and representative works.

Unit 4: *Musical Instruments and the Voice* provides knowledge of and insight into the characteristic sounds of band, orchestra, folk instruments, and the voice.

Unit 5: *Great Composers and Their Music* familiarizes the student with some of the foremost composers of the past and present and their music; and cultivates an early taste for good music.

Unit 6: *Special Days Throughout the Year* offers the student well-illustrated, music-related activities that stimulate interest and discussion about music through holidays and special occasions for the entire school year.

Unit 7: *Musicians in Action* helps the student examine music as a pastime or for a career by exploring daily encounters with music and the skills, duties, environment, and requirements of a variety of careers in music.

How to Use the *Library*

The activities in each Unit of the *Library* may be sequenced and developed in different ways. The general teacher may want to use one activity after the other, while the music specialist may prefer to use the activities in conjunction with the sequencing of the music curriculum. Teachers with special or individualized needs may select activities from various Units and use them over and over before actually introducing new material.

Let's take a closer look at how you can use the *Music Curriculum Activities Library* in your particular classroom situation:

... For THE MUSIC TEACHER who is accountable for teaching classes at many grade levels, there is a wide range of activities with varying degrees of difficulty. The activity sheets are ideal to strengthen and review skills and concepts suitable for the general music class.

... For THE NEW TEACHER STARTING A GENERAL MUSIC CLASS, these fun-filled activities will provide a well-balanced, concrete core program.

... For THE SPECIALIZED TEACHER who needs to set definite teaching goals, these activities offer a wealth of information about certain areas of music, such as career awareness, composers, and musical forms.

... For THE BAND AND CHOIR DIRECTOR, these activity sheets are a valuable resource to explore band, orchestra, and folk instruments, along with the singing voice.

... For THE PRIVATE MUSIC TEACHER who wants to sharpen and improve students' note reading skills, the *Library* offers ample homework assignments to give students the additional practice they need. There are many activity sheets using the clef of one's instrument and theory pages with illustrations of the keyboard.

... For THE MUSIC CONSULTANT using any one of the units, there are plenty of activities specifically correlated to the various areas of music providing reinforcement of learning. The activity sheets are suitable for class adoption in correlation with any music book series.

... For THE THEORY TEACHER, there are activities to show the students that music analysis is fun and easy.

... For THE TEACHER WHO NEEDS AN ADEQUATE MEANS OF EVALUATING STUDENT PROGRESS, there are fact-filled activities ideal for diagnostic purposes. A space is provided on each sheet for a score to be given.

. . . For THE CLASSROOM TEACHER with little or no musical background, the *Library* offers effective teaching with the flexibility of the seven units. All that has to be done is to decide on the music skill or concept to be taught and then duplicate the necessary number of copies. Even the answers can be duplicated for self-checking.

. . . For THE SUBSTITUTE TEACHER, these sheets are ideal for seatwork assignments because the directions are generally self-explanatory with minimal supervision required.

. . . For THE INSTRUCTOR OF GIFTED STUDENTS, the activities may be used for any type of independent, individualized instruction and learning centers. When used in an individualized fashion, the gifted student has an opportunity to pursue music learning at his or her own pace.

. . . For THE TEACHER OF SPECIAL EDUCATION, even the disadvantaged and remedial student can get in on the fun. Each concept or skill will be mastered as any lesson may be repeated or reinforced with another activity. Some of these activity sheets are designed to provide success for students who have difficulty in other subject areas.

. . . For the INDIVIDUAL who desires to broaden and expand his or her own knowledge and interest in music, each Unit provides 50 activities to help enjoy music.

The *Music Curriculum Activities Library* is ideally a teacher's program because a minimum of planning is required. A quick glance at the Contents in each Unit reveals the titles of all the activity sheets, the ability level necessary to use them, and the skills involved for each student. Little knowledge of music is generally needed to introduce the lessons, and extensive preparation is seldom necessary. You will, of course, want to read through the activity before presenting it to the class. In cases where you need to give information about the activity, two different approaches might be considered. (1) Use the activity as a basis for a guided discussion before completing the activity to achieve the desired results, or (2) Use the activity as a foundation for a lesson plan and then follow up by completing the activity. Either one of these approaches will enhance your own and your students' confidence and, by incorporating a listening or performing experience with this directed study, the students will have a well-rounded daily lesson.

All activity sheets throughout the *Library* have the same format. They are presented in an uncluttered, easy-to-read fashion, with self-explanatory directions. You need no extra materials or equipment, except for an occasional pair of scissors. The classroom or resource area should, however, contain a few reference books, such as song books or music series' books, encyclopedias, reference books about composers, a dictionary, music dictionary or glossary, and so on, so that while working on certain activities the student has easy access to resource books. Then, you simply need to duplicate the activity sheet as many times as needed and give a copy to each student. Even paper grading can be kept to a minimum by reproducing the answer key for self-checking.

The collection of activities includes practice in classifying, matching, listing, researching, naming, drawing, decoding, identifying, doing picture or crossword puzzles, anagrams, word searches, musical word squares, and much much more.

These materials may be used successfully with students in grades 3 and up. The activities and artwork are intentionally structured to appeal to a wide range of ages. For this reason, no grade-level references appear on the activity sheets so that you can use them in a variety of classroom settings, although suggested ability levels (beginner, intermediate, advanced) appear in the Contents.

The potential uses for the *Library* for any musical purpose (or even interdisciplinary study) are countless. Why? Because these activities allow you to instruct an entire class, a smaller group within the classroom, or individual students. While you are actively engaged in teaching one group of students, the activity sheets may be completed by another group. In any kind of classroom setting, even with the gifted music student or the remedial child, no student needs to sit idle. Now you will have more time for individual instruction.

The Units may be used in a comprehensive music skills program, in an enrichment program, or even in a remedial program. The *Library* is perfect for building a comprehensive musicianship program, improving basic music skills, teaching career awareness, building music vocabulary, exploring instruments, developing good taste in listening to music, appreciating different types of music, creating a positive learning environment, and providing growing confidence in the performer.

What Each Unit Offers You

A quick examination of the **Contents** will reveal a well balanced curriculum. Included are the titles of all activities, the level of difficulty, and the skill involved. The exception to this is Unit 6, where the date and special day, rather than the skill, are listed with the title of each activity.

Each of the **50 reproducible activity sheets** generally presents a single idea, with a consistent format and easy-to-follow directions on how to do the activity, along with a sufficient amount of material to enable the student to become proficient through independent and self-directed work. Because each activity has but one single behavioral objective, mastery of each skill builds confidence that allows the learner to continue progressively toward a more complete understanding of the structure of music, appreciation of music, and its uses. The activity sheets are just the right length, too, designed to be completed within a class period.

The **Progress Chart** provides a uniform, objective method of determining what skills have been mastered. With the aid of this chart, you will be able to keep track of goals, set priorities, organize daily and weekly lesson plans, and track assignments. The Progress Chart lists each activity and skill involved, and has a space for individual names or classes to be recorded and checked when each activity and skill is complete. The Progress Chart is ideal for accurate record keeping. It provides a quick, sure method for you to determine each individual student's achievements or weaknesses.

Use the **Teacher's Guide** for practical guidance on how the particular Unit will work for you. An easy effective learning system, this guide provides background information and reveals new techniques for teaching the Unit.

Throughout the *Library*, each **Answer Key** is designed with a well-thought-out system for checking students' answers. While some activities are self-checking without the use of the Answer Key, other activities can easily be student corrected, too, by simply duplicating the answer page and cutting apart the answers by activity number.

The **Self-Improvement Chart** provides the student with a self-assessment system that links curriculum goals with individual goals. By means of an appraisal checklist, the chart gives the student and teacher alike the key to finding individual talent. It also measures accountability. Included in the chart are (1) a method for recording goals and acquired music skills; (2) a log for attendance at special music events; (3) a music and instrument check-out record; (4) a log for extra credit activities and music projects; (5) a record of special music recognition awards, incentive badges, Music Share-a-Grams, Return-a-Grams; and (6) a record of music progress.

These specific features of the chart will help you:

- Provide a uniform, objective method of determining rewards for students.
- Assess future curriculum needs by organizing long-term information on student performance.
- Foster understanding of why students did or did not qualify for additional merit.
- Motivate students by giving them feedback on ways for self-improvement.
- Assist students in making statements of their own desires and intentions for learning, and in checking progress toward their goals.

The **Music Share-a-Gram** is a personalized progress report addressed to the parent and created to show the unique qualities of the individual child. It allows you to pinpoint areas of success and tell parents what they need to know about their child. The Music Share-a-Gram evaluates twelve important abilities and personal traits with ratings from exceptional to unsatisfactory, which you might want to discuss with students to solicit their reaction. For example, you might use these ratings as a basis for selecting a student to attend the gifted program in music. This form is designed to be sent with or without the Return-a-Gram, and may be hand-delivered by the student or sent through the mail. For easy record keeping, make a copy of the Gram and attach it to the back of the Student Record Profile Chart.

The **Return-a-Gram** is designed to accompany the Music Share-a-Gram and is sent to the parent on special occasions. When a reply is not expected or necessary, simply detach the Return-a-Gram before sending the Share-a-Gram. This form encourages feedback from the parent and even allows the parent to arrange for a parent-teacher conference. Both Grams are printed on the same page and are self-explanatory—complete with a dotted line for the parent to detach, fill in, and return.

The **Student Record Profile Chart** is a guide for understanding and helping students, and offers a means of periodic evaluation. The chart is easy to use and provides all you need for accurate record keeping and measuring accountability for individual student progress throughout all seven units. It provides an accumulative skills profile for the student and represents an actual score of his or her written performance for each activity. Here is a workable form that you can immediately tailor to your own requirements for interpretation and use of scores. Included are clear instructions, with an example, to help you record your students' assessment on a day-to-day basis, to keep track of pupil progress, and to check learning patterns over a period of time. This chart allows you to spot the potential superior achiever along with the remedial individual. The chart coordinates all aspects of data ranging from the students' name, class, school, classroom teacher's name, semester, date, page number, actual grade, and attendance.

The **Word List** is presented as a reinforcement for building a music vocabulary. It emphasizes the use of dictionary skills; the students make a glossary of important words related to the particular unit. Its purpose is to encourage the use of vocabulary skills by helping develop an understanding of the music terms, concepts, and names found on the activity sheets. This vocabulary reference page is meant to be reproduced and used by the individual student throughout the units as a guide for spelling, word recognition, pronunciation, recording definitions, plus any other valuable information. Throughout six units of the *Library*, a cumulation of the words are presented on the Word List pages. (A Word List is not included in Unit 6.) With the help of this extensive vocabulary, when the student uses the words on both the activity page and the Word List, they will become embedded as part of his or her language.

Each Unit contains a wide-ranging collection of **Incentive Badges**. Use them to reward excellence, commend effort, for bonuses, prizes, behavior modification, or as reminders. These badges are designed to capture the interest and attention of the entire school. Several badges are designed with an open-ended format to provide maximum flexibility in meeting any special music teaching requirement.

Included in each Unit is a simple **Craft Project** that may be created by the entire class or by individual students. Each craft project is an integral part of the subject matter of that particular unit and will add a rich dimension to the activities. The materials necessary for the construction of the craft projects have been limited to those readily available in most classrooms and call for no special technical or artistic skills.

PLUS each Unit contains:

- Worked-out sample problems for students to use as a standard and model for their own work.

- Additional teaching suggestions in the Answer Key for getting the most out of certain activities.

- Extra staff paper for unlimited use, such as composing, ear training, improvising, or writing chords.

- Activities arranged in a sequential pattern.

Resources for Teaching Music More Effectively

- Have a classroom dictionary available for reference.
- Have a glossary or music dictionary available for reference.
- Use only one activity sheet per class session.
- Distribute the Word List prior to the first activity sheet of the particular unit. Encourage students to underline familiar words on the list and write definitions or identifications on the back before instruction on the unit begins. Later, the students can compare their answers with those studied.
- Provide short-term goals for each class session and inform students in advance that awards will be given for the day. You'll see how their conduct improves, too.
- Encourage students to make or buy an inexpensive folder to store music activity sheets, craft projects, word lists, self-evaluation charts, and so on. Folders might be kept in the classroom when not in use and distributed at the beginning of each class period.
- Many of the activities are ideal for bulletin board display. If space is not available to display all students' work, rotate the exhibits.
- Encourage students to re-read creative writing pages for clarity and accuracy before copying the final form on the activity sheet. Proofreading for grammatical and spelling errors should be encouraged.
- For creative drawing activities, encourage students to sketch their initial ideas on another sheet of paper first, then draw the finished product on the activity sheet. It is not necessary to have any technical ability in drawing to experience the pleasure of these creative activities.
- Although you will probably want to work through parts of some activities with your students, and choose some activities for group projects, you will find that most lessons are designed to lead students to the correct answers with little or no teacher direction. Students can be directed occasionally to work through an activity with a partner to search out and correct specific errors.
- Self-corrections and self-checking make a much better impression on young learners than do red-penciled corrections by the classroom music teacher.
- On activities where answers will vary, encourage students to rate their own work on correctness, originality, completeness, carefulness, realism, and organization.

• Most activity pages will serve as a "teacher assistant" in developing specific skills or subject areas to study. The activities throughout the series are complete with learning objectives and are generally factual enough for the teacher to use as a basis for a daily lesson plan.

• The library research activities promote creativity instead of copying while students search out relevant data from a variety of sources, such as encyclopedias, dictionaries, reference books, autobiographies, and others. These activities are ideal for the individual student or groups of students working beyond the classroom environment.

• The following are practical guidelines in planning, organizing, and constructing the Craft Projects:

> . . . Acquaint yourself with any of the techniques that are new to you before you ask your students to undertake the project.
>
> . . . Decide on your project and assemble the materials before you begin.
>
> . . . Make a sample model for experience.
>
> . . . Use a flat surface for working.
>
> . . . Be sure the paper is cut exactly to measurements and that folds are straight.
>
> . . . Be available for consultation.
>
> . . . Provide guidance on what the next logical step is to encourage all students to finish their projects.
>
> . . . Use the finished craft projects as displays and points of interest for your school's open house.

• Many of the Incentive Badges found in each Unit are open-ended and can be made effective communication tools to meet your needs. Extra space is provided on these badges for additional written messages that might be used for any number of reasons. Be creative for your own special needs; load the copier with colored paper and print as many as you need for the semester or entire school year. Then simply use a paper cutter to separate the badges and sort them out alphabetically. Make an alphabetical index on file card dividers using these titles. Next, arrange them in an accessible file box or shoe box, depending on the size needed. Include a roll of tape to attach the badge to the recipient.

Teacher's Guide to Unit 3

The primary purpose of *Musical Form and Composition* is to stimulate music listening in the classroom through enrichment activities, and to help give children the foundation they need to enjoy worthwhile music. Its 50 activities help bridge the gap between popular and classical music by covering such types of music as bluegrass, barbershop, musicals, patriotic, spirituals, folk, and symphonic forms. The activities help students understand their cultural and traditional music heritage, while helping you capture the interest of *every* student.

You will discover much about your students' interests, music background, and prior knowledge of different music forms by presenting the first activity sheet, "Interest Inventory." After assessing the background of the class, you will be better able to select initial activities suitable for that class. Several activities in the first section guide young people to relate to their own musical experiences and their environment through classification. A walking field trip around the schoolyard, for example, might provide enough incentive for students to begin categorizing various sounds.

The activities in Unit 3 are multidisciplinary and can be used with lessons in history, spelling, reading, art, and geography. Activity 3-9, for example, can be used in conjunction with American history while studying the way of life in the early frontier. Discuss why, when, and what type of songs cowboys sang. Then, after singing a few cowboy songs or listening to cowboy music, you can conclude the lesson with the activity sheet.

The creative drawing and writing activities can be used to show how music is an integral part of everyday life. Have the class list or discuss the different types of music heard every day, such as radio commercials, television jingles, school assemblies, concerts, weddings, funerals, religious services, parades, movies, waiting rooms, and sports events. When completed, activity sheets 3-10 through 3-14 provide an attractive visual display on the bulletin board or make an interesting collective scrap book.

Activities 3-15 through 3-20 deal with dance and jazz. You could introduce the word "ethnic" and lead your students to discover how each country or section of a country has its own customs and rituals, including native dances.

The library research sections allow you to offer independent study to a small group or individual students. Some of these activities may be completed during classroom time if suitable resources are available. For example, if there is a supply of any music series books, "Learning Our National Anthem" could be used as an enrichment lesson.

Musicals and operas, as well as popular music, religious music, and spirituals, are explored so that students can relate musical life within the community to the musical experiences within the school. Motivate the students to attend local performances or watch events on television or at the movies. Follow up with one of the corresponding activity sheets.

Also presented in Unit 3 are symphonic forms, which should be correlated to active listening. Teach your students proper audience behavior by explaining what it really means to listen. Insist that there be no talking, writing, or reading while the students listen attentively. Try to create music lovers and future concert-goers through your motivation and enthusiasm. Do not let these activities be a means in themselves, but a means to enjoy classical music.

Because music appreciation is an integral part of any music program, stress that music listening, performing within the classroom, and/or attending concerts should always go hand-in-hand with the activities in Unit 3. Because of the nature of these activity sheets, specific listening assignments are left to your discretion.

Contents

Activity Number/Title	Skill Involved	Level of Difficulty
Children's Music		
3-1 INTEREST INVENTORY	Taking a personal assessment to determine own favorite type of music	Beginner
3-2 QUESTIONS FROM THE SITTER	Recalling facts about nursery songs	Beginner
3-3 WHAT DO YOU HEAR?	Listing and classifying indoor sounds according to loud and soft	Beginner
3-4 CLASSIFY THE SOUNDS	Listing and classifying outdoor sounds according to loud and soft	Beginner
3-5 WHAT'S THAT SOUND?	Classifying country and city sounds by types, origins, and descriptions	Beginner
3-6 ENTER THE SINGING GAME CONTEST	Creating a musical game	Beginner
3-7 A DISNEY QUIZ	Matching Disney songs with productions	Beginner
Country-Western		
3-8 THE COUNTRY SCRAMBLE	Recalling facts about country music	Beginner
Cowboy Songs		
3-9 IDENTIFY THE COWBOY SONGS	Matching titles of cowboy songs with beginning words and notes	Beginner

Contents

Contents   xix

Activity Number/Title	Skill Involved	Level of Difficulty
Spirituals		
3–41 WRITE THE LYRICS	Writing the lyrics for beginning bars of five well-known spirituals	Intermediate
Symphonic Forms		
3–42 CONCERTO CLUES	Using a code to identify terms relating to a concerto	Beginner
3–43 MATCH THE DATES	Using a puzzle square to match dates with periods in history	Beginner
3–44 SPELL IT WITH NOTES	Naming various forms of music using a note code and matching with definitions	Beginner
3–45 UNSCRAMBLE AND MATCH	Unscrambling names of symphonic forms to match definitions	Beginner
3–46 FINISH THE CANON	Finishing a canon using notation on a treble staff	Intermediate
3–47 TACKLE THE TITLE	Matching descriptions of program music with titles	Intermediate
3–48 SONATA-ALLEGRO FORM WORD SEARCH	Completing sentences about sonata-allegro form	Intermediate
3–49 ANALYZE THE FORM	Analyzing "The Marines' Hymn" as Three Part Song Form (AABA)	Intermediate
3–50 MAKING ALPHABET SOUP	Classifying various forms of composition	Intermediate

Activities for Learning About CHILDREN'S MUSIC

INTEREST INVENTORY   3–1

1. My favorite type of music is _____

_____.

2. I know about these different types of music:

_____

_____

_____

_____

_____

_____

_____

_____

3. The type of music I would like to learn more about is _____.

4. My favorite place to listen to music is _____.

5. I feel happy when I listen to _____

_____.

6. I listen to music most when I feel _____.

7. I'd rather listen to music than _____

_____.

8. My favorite musical group is _____.

9. My favorite record album is _____.

10. My favorite radio station is _____.

11. My favorite song is _____.

12. To me, music is _____

_____

_____.

Name _____   Score _____

Date _____   Class _____

QUESTIONS FROM THE SITTER   3-2

Pretend you are baby sitting. You have been entertaining the children by singing nursery rhymes until you are "blue in the face." You decide to do something else, so you ask the children if they would like to play "nursery questions." They all say, "Yes, yes." Here are their questions. Underline the correct answers.

1. Where was rock-a-bye baby?
   a. in a cradle
   b. in a hammock
   c. in a buggy

2. What kind of person was Old King Cole?
   a. grumpy
   b. mean
   c. merry

3. In the song "Bye Baby Bunting" what has daddy gone to get the baby?
   a. a bottle
   b. a sleeper
   c. a little rabbit skin

4. Why did the last little piggy cry?
   a. He was upset.
   b. He couldn't find his way home.
   c. He was hungry.

5. In "Rub-a-dub-dub" where were the three men?
   a. in a tub
   b. in a pub
   c. in a sub

6. Where did the mouse run?
   a. up the clock
   b. up the street
   c. up the wall

7. "Twinkle, twinkle little star how I wonder . . ."
   a. where you are
   b. who you are
   c. what you are

8. Down came the rain and washed the
   a. kettle out
   b. dirt away
   c. spider out

9. Tom, Tom, the piper's son stole a
   a. bun
   b. pig
   c. dime

10. Who went "Pop?"
    a. the rabbit
    b. the weasel
    c. the jack-in-the box

11. What did Polly do?
    a. hold the teddy bear
    b. put the kettle down
    c. put the kettle on

12. Where is
    a. Thumbkin?
    b. Bumpkin?
    c. Pumpkin?

WHAT DO YOU HEAR?   3–3

Listen indoors for the different sounds you hear. Use this chart to record your findings. Classify the sounds according to loud sounds or soft sounds.

LOUD SOUNDS	SOFT SOUNDS

Name _____   Score _____

Date _____   Class _____

CLASSIFY THE SOUNDS   3–4

Listen outdoors for the different sounds you hear. Use this chart to record your findings. Classify the sounds according to loud sounds or soft sounds.

LOUD SOUNDS	SOFT SOUNDS

WHAT'S THAT SOUND? 3–5

What kinds of sounds do you hear every day? List as many sounds as you can think of, along with the origin and a description of the sound. Think about the different types of sounds in the country and in the city. Two examples are provided.

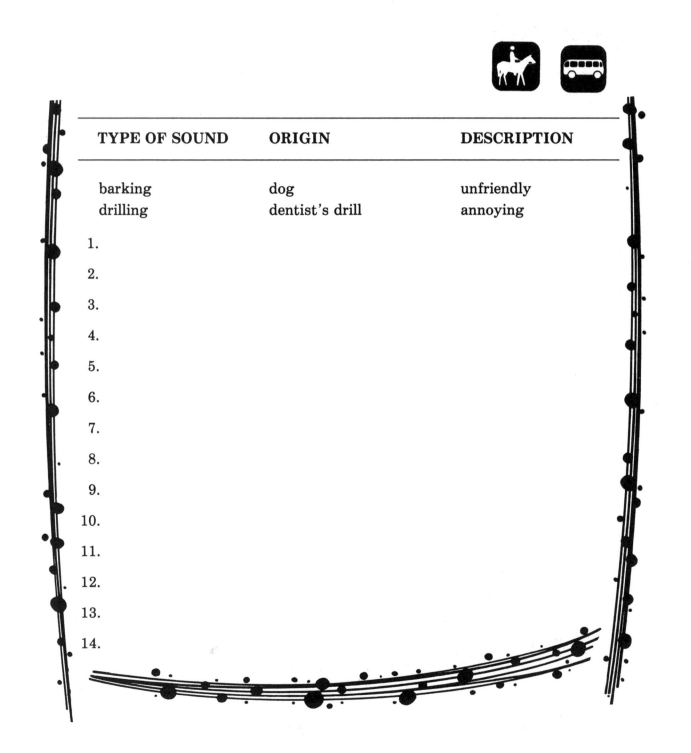

TYPE OF SOUND	ORIGIN	DESCRIPTION
barking	dog	unfriendly
drilling	dentist's drill	annoying
1.		
2.		
3.		
4.		
5.		
6.		
7.		
8.		
9.		
10.		
11.		
12.		
13.		
14.		

ENTER THE SINGING GAME CONTEST   3–6

Think of all the games you've played that were based on a song you sang. You have probably heard of singing games like "The Hokey Pokey" and "London Bridge." Name another singing game that you know.

_____

Pretend that you have been asked by your P.T.O. president to enter the school contest to invent a singing game. The winner will play his or her singing game with the school children during the meeting of the P.T.O. Use a melody from a song you already know, but not one from the songs mentioned above. Then, decide on the type of game to play. Write new words (lyrics) to the song. Remember, there may be children of different ages, so keep it simple. Use the format below. Your game will be judged by how well you have combined the music, words, and choreography.

TITLE OF THE GAME: _____

BY: _____

OBJECT OF THE GAME:

WORDS TO THE SONG: (To be sung to the tune of _____

_____.)

DIRECTIONS TO PLAY THE GAME: (Use the back of this sheet.)

A DISNEY QUIZ   3–7

Find the Disney production that goes with each song in the list. Write the number of the song in the matching Mickey Mouse hat.

1. "A Spoonful of Sugar"
2. "The Bare Necessities"
3. "Bibbidi-Bobbidi-Boo"
4. "Following the Leader"
5. "Home on the Range"
6. "March of the Toys"
7. "The Siamese Cat Song"
8. "The Unbirthday Song"

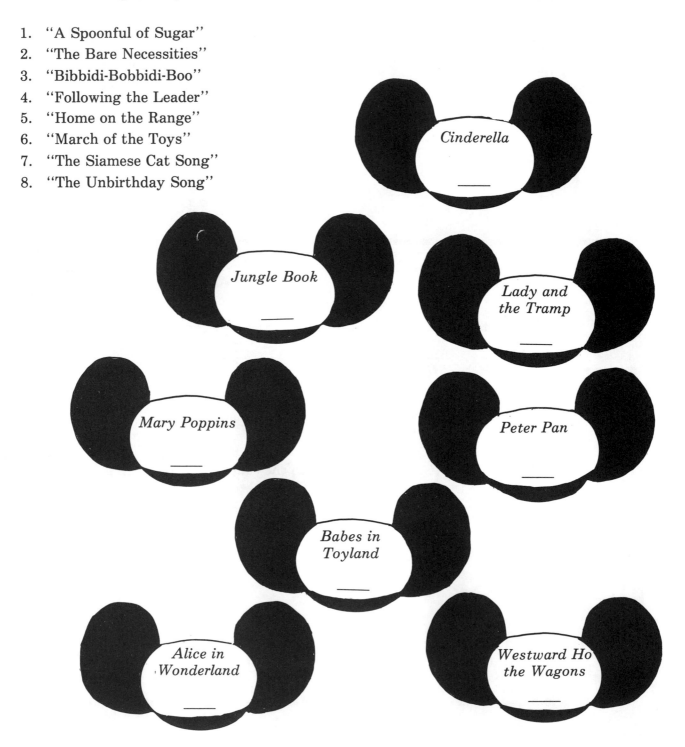

Activity for Learning About
COUNTRY-WESTERN

3-8   **THE COUNTRY SCRAMBLE**

Name _____   Score _____

Date _____   Class _____

THE COUNTRY SCRAMBLE   3–8

The scrambled words under the blanks are your answers for these questions about country music.

1. Another name for country music:

   _____
   RUNTOYC   NEWSRET

2. Country music emphasizes this instrument:

   _____
   RIGATU

3. The most popular kind of music in the United States:

   _____
   TOYCUNR

4. What city (and state) is the center of publishing and recording country music?

   _____
   LINEVSHAL,   NESENETES

5. The "King" of country music: _____
                                   YOR   CAFUF

6. What instrument did Earl Scruggs use to play country music? He invented special tuning pegs, plus the use of a thumb pick and two to three finger picks for this instrument.

   _____
   JANBO

7. The name of a well-known country song:

   _____
   ???

8. Where you would go to see the best country performers on stage:

   _____
   DRANG   LOD   PROY

9. A type of country music played on stringed instruments, without any percussion instruments:

   _____
   LUBERAGSS

10. The father of bluegrass: _____
                               LLIB   RONOME

Activity for Learning About
COWBOY SONGS

3-9   **IDENTIFY THE COWBOY SONGS**

Name _____   Score _____

Date _____   Class _____

IDENTIFY THE COWBOY SONGS  3–9

Here are the beginning measures of five well-known cowboy songs. Guess the title of each song and write it on the blank under the staff. If you need additional clues, listed at the bottom of the page are several popular cowboy songs from which you can choose.

From this val - ley they say you are go - ing.___ We will

1. _____

As I was a - walk -in' one morn- ing for

2. _____

Oh give me a home where the buf - fa - lo

3. _____

My home's in Mon - tan - a, I wear a ban-

4. _____

As I walked out in the streets of La - re -do, As

5. _____

. . . .

"Yellow Rose of Texas"   "My Home's in Montana"   "Happy Trails"
"The Streets of Laredo"   "Jessie James"   "Git Along, Little Dogies"
"Red River Valley"   "I Ride an Old Paint"   "Frankie and Johnny"
"Ol' Texas"   "Home on the Range"   "The Dying Cowboy"

Activities for Learning About
CREATIVE DRAWING

Name _____   Score _____

Date _____   Class _____

JUST DAYDREAMING   3–10

We all have fun sitting and daydreaming sometimes. If you could be listening to your favorite type of music, what would you choose? Draw a picture that shows it.

YOU DRAW IT   3-11

In each of the boxes, draw a sketch to illustrate a type of music. Choose from the list below. Do not label your drawings. Make each picture detailed enough so that someone looking at it would be able to identify the type of music. Use your own ideas and make your drawings original. On the back of the page, list in order the types of music you sketched.

barbershop quartet, ballet, band, chorus, country western, jazz, musical, opera, orchestra, religious, rock, other . . .

Activities for Learning About CREATIVE WRITING

Name _____ Score _____

Date _____ Class _____

MY FAVORITE TYPE OF MUSIC IS... 3–12

Imagine you have been asked to write an article for your school paper. Write a paragraph of five or six sentences explaining what your favorite type of music is and why. Include some titles of favorite tunes and also names of performers that you like. Make your story interesting.

WRITE A COVER STORY   3–13

You are asked to submit an article about a musical event you will be attending. Include the name of the event, date, location, and what was performed. During the performance take notes, writing down your opinions, impressions, and reactions to the music. Also say something about the quality of music using terms such as, pitch, rhythm, tempo, volume or timbre. Copy your article in the space below. Use the back of the page if needed.

Name _____   Score _____

Date _____   Class _____

YOU'RE THE CRITIC   3-14

You're the critic for the local newspaper. Write a review for
the musical event you most recently attended. Include the
type of program you attended, who performed, the date, what
music was performed, and what you liked and didn't like
about the performance and why.

_____

_____

_____

_____

_____

_____

_____

_____

_____

_____

_____

_____

_____

_____

_____

_____

_____

_____

_____

Activities for Learning About
DANCE

DIAL A DANCE

3–15

Use the telephone dial to find out the names of these national dances of the 19th and 20th century. The beginning letter of each dance is given as a clue.

1. Bohemian
$$\frac{P}{7} \ \frac{}{6} \ \frac{}{5} \ \frac{}{5} \ \frac{}{2}$$

2. Polish
$$\frac{M}{6} \ \frac{}{2} \ \frac{}{0} \ \frac{}{8} \ \frac{}{7} \ \frac{}{5} \ \frac{}{2}$$

3. Italian
$$\frac{T}{8} \ \frac{}{2} \ \frac{}{7} \ \frac{}{2} \ \frac{}{6} \ \frac{}{8} \ \frac{}{3} \ \frac{}{5} \ \frac{}{5} \ \frac{}{2}$$

4. Viennese
$$\frac{W}{9} \ \frac{}{2} \ \frac{}{5} \ \frac{}{8} \ \frac{}{0}$$

5. Cuban
$$\frac{B}{2} \ \frac{}{6} \ \frac{}{5} \ \frac{}{3} \ \frac{}{7} \ \frac{}{6}$$

6. Spanish
$$\frac{H}{4} \ \frac{}{2} \ \frac{}{2} \ \frac{}{2} \ \frac{}{6} \ \frac{}{3} \ \frac{}{7} \ \frac{}{2}$$

7. Argentine
$$\frac{T}{8} \ \frac{}{2} \ \frac{}{6} \ \frac{}{4} \ \frac{}{6}$$

8. American
$$\frac{D}{3} \ \frac{}{4} \ \frac{}{7} \ \frac{}{2} \ \frac{}{6}$$

DABBLING IN DANCE

ACROSS

1. Each kind of dance uses a certain kind of ____.
3. ____ dancing, a highly rhythmic dance requires slippers with cleats.
4. ____ dances have been passed down from generation to generation.
8. Italian march.
9. A quick Italian dance named after a poisonous spider.
10. The word comes from the English "Jig." A fast sailor's dance.
13. There are seven steps in every musical ____.
14. A classical French dance in $\frac{2}{2}$ time.
15. An Argentine Dance.
17. (Fr.) A quick dance in triple time.
18. A dance with three beats to the bar.
21. A Cuban dance popular in the U.S.A. from about 1930; probably of African origin.
23. Popular dance of the 1970s.
24. A Bohemian dance in quick duple time.
25. ____ dancing includes national, racial, primitive and folk dancing of all people.
26. ____nome: an instrument used as an aid for keeping time.
27. ____ dancing originated in the courts of Europe.

DOWN

2. In a ____ dance every dancer has an opportunity to dance with other dancers in his or her group.
3. Fox ____ is a name given to a ballroom dance.
5. Broad and dignified. (It.)
6. A dance originally from France, later popular in Britain.

(Down)

7. A formal dance in which the dancer keeps a rigid torso.
8. Polish dance in triple time with accent on second beat.
11. A mid-19th century round dance.
12. A lively Spanish dance.
16. Originally a French dance that became very popular in the 18th century.
19. Dancers use free expressive movements in this dance.
20. It takes much ____ to become a good dancer.
22. The big dance ____ era was popular in the early 1940s.

Activities for Learning About
FOLK SONGS

Name _____   Score _____

Date _____   Class _____

FINISH THE TITLES   3–17

These American folk songs are all missing the last word from their titles. Find the answers in the map below and write the answers in the blanks.

1. THE BEAR WENT OVER THE _____

2. BUFFALO _____

3. GO TELL AUNT _____

4. DOWN IN THE _____

5. DRILL, YE TARRIERS, _____

6. JOHN _____

7. LONG, LONG _____

8. PAPER OF _____

9. SOLDIER, SOLDIER, WON'T YOU MARRY _____

10. SWEET BETSY FROM _____

Name _____   Score _____

Date _____   Class _____

WHAT'S NEXT?

Here are the beginning measures of five great American folk songs. The last note of each example is missing. Draw in the missing note at the end of each staff. The notes to choose from are at the bottom of this sheet.

1. She'll Be Comin' 'Round the Mountain

She'll be com-in' 'round the moun-tain when she comes _____ She'll be

2. Skip to My Lou

Lost my part-ner what'll I do? Lost my part-ner what'll I do?

3. Hush, Little Baby

Hush, Lit-tle Ba-by, don't say a word, Pa-pa's gon-na buy you a mock-ing bird,

4. Red River Valley

From this val - ley they say you are go - ing. _____ I will

5. Yankee Doodle

Fath'r and I went down to camp, A-long with Cap-tain Good-win, And there we saw the

NOTES TO CHOOSE FROM:

a.   b.   c.   d.   e.

Activities for Learning About
CHILDREN'S MUSIC

Name _____   Score _____

Date _____   Class _____

RIFFS, LICKS, AND CHOPS   3–19

Test your knowledge of jazz music. See how many of your answers you can write on the blanks below without referring to the key at the bottom of the page.

1. What type of music gets its influence from African, Eastern, folk and country music?

   _____.

2. How many primary chords are usually used in jazz? _____.

3. How many bars are there in this typical blues pattern? (The letters representing the chords

   are in the key of C.)   CCCCFFCCGFCC _____.

4. When the third and seventh scale degrees are lowered to make the blues scale, what are

   these notes called? _____.

5. The blues has a definite form consisting of three four-measure _____.

6. The _____ is usually slow and steady in blues music.

7. A musical phrase that is repeated for a whole section of a song and is frequently played on

   guitar and bass is called _____.

8. Jargon used to describe a musical phrase _____ _____.

9. A jazz vernacular when a performer has great skill on an instrument—_____

10. When a musician performs spontaneously without the aid of memorization or notation, it

    is called _____.

11. Vocal improvisation without words is called _____ singing.

12. Another word for improvisation is _____.

1. jazz	7. riff
2. three	8. lick
3. twelve	9. chops
4. blue	10. improvisation
5. phrases	11. scat
6. tempo	12. ad libbing

DECODE THE NICKNAMES

3-20

Throughout history we have known different jazz musicians by their nicknames. Use the secret code to write the nicknames of these jazz artists. The number 1 note matches the number 1 blank in the name. Write the letter names of the notes to complete the nicknames.

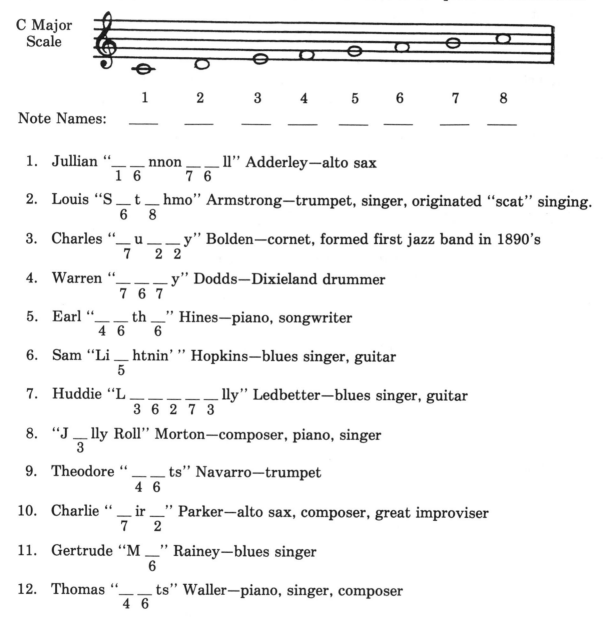

C Major Scale

1 2 3 4 5 6 7 8

Note Names: ___ ___ ___ ___ ___ ___ ___ ___

1. Jullian "__ __ nnon __ __ ll" Adderley—alto sax
    1 6   7 6

2. Louis "S __ t __ hmo" Armstrong—trumpet, singer, originated "scat" singing.
         6   8

3. Charles "__ u __ __ y" Bolden—cornet, formed first jazz band in 1890's
            7   2 2

4. Warren "__ __ __ y" Dodds—Dixieland drummer
           7 6 7

5. Earl "__ __ th __" Hines—piano, songwriter
         4 6   6

6. Sam "Li __ htnin'" Hopkins—blues singer, guitar
            5

7. Huddie "L __ __ __ __ __ lly" Ledbetter—blues singer, guitar
              3 6 2 7 3

8. "J __ lly Roll" Morton—composer, piano, singer
       3

9. Theodore "__ __ ts" Navarro—trumpet
             4 6

10. Charlie "__ ir __" Parker—alto sax, composer, great improviser
             7   2

11. Gertrude "M __" Rainey—blues singer
                6

12. Thomas "__ __ ts" Waller—piano, singer, composer
            4 6

Activities for Learning About
LIBRARY RESEARCH

WHICH TYPE IS IT?   3–21

Each group of songs in the frame is classified as one of the following types of music:

P = PATRIOTIC SONGS   S = SPIRITUALS
R = ROUNDS AND CANONS   C = SEA SONGS AND CHANTIES

Decide what type of music each group is. Then write the letter of type on the blank. Draw a + sign after the titles that you know.

a. ____
Frère Jacques
Kookaburra
Oh, How Lovely Is the Evening
Row, Row, Row Your Boat

b. ____
Get on Board Little Children
Go Tell It on the Mountain
My Lord What a Mornin'
Nobody Knows the Trouble I've Seen

c. ____
Blow the Man Down
Over the Waves
Rio Grande
Sailing, Sailing

d. ____
America the Beautiful
The Battle Hymn of the Republic
I'm a Yankee Doodle Dandy
The Star Spangled Banner

MARCH TO THE LIBRARY

Answer the following questions. Use a reference book if you need help.

1. Define the word "march." _____.

   _____

   _____

2. At what events do we hear marches? _____.

   _____

   _____

3. Who is the most famous composer of marches and what is his title?

   _____   _____

               (name)   (title)

4. About how many marches did John Philip Sousa write? _____

5. What is the name of your favorite march? _____

   _____

6. What is the name of your favorite marching band? _____

   _____

Name _____   Score _____

Date _____   Class _____

LEARNING OUR NATIONAL ANTHEM   3–23

USE A #2 PENCIL !!

With a copy of the words and music of our national anthem in front of you, read each of the following questions. Circle your answers.

1. What is the name of our national anthem?
   a. "God Bless America"   b. "America the Beautiful"
               c. "The Star-Spangled Banner"

2. Who wrote the words to our national anthem?
   a. Francis Scott Key   b. Katherine Lee Bates
               c. Author unknown

3. What do these words in the first verse of "The Star-Spangled Banner" mean?
   hailed   a. small pieces of ice   b. a state of suffering   c. shout in welcome to
   perilous   a. white gem   b. dangerous   c. long
   ramparts   a. violence   b. parade   c. a wide bank of earth built around a fort
   gallantly a. bravely and nobly   b. brilliantly   c. happily

4. Which melody line in the song looks and sounds like the first line?
   a. fourth   b. last   c. third

5. Which melody line looks and sounds like the second line?
   a. third   b. fourth   c. fifth

6. Over what word in the song is there a fermata (⌒)?
   a. home   b. land   c. wave

7. Where does the song slightly ritard?
   a. last line   b. first line   c. third line

8. What is the most important word in the song?
   a. free   b. wave   c. flag

9. How many phrases are there in the song?
   a. four   b. two   c. eight

10. What is the form of this song?
    a. AABC   b. ABA   c. Rondo

Use the back of this page to answer the following:

11. List two ways to show expressions of patriotism while singing our national anthem.

12. Use a reference book to learn about the events that inspired the writing of the national anthem. Explain how the author wrote the words for this song.

FIND THE RESOURCE   3–24

Imagine that you are in the library to look up this information. The resources are listed at the bottom of the page. Opposite the information, write the resource you would use.

_____   1. The page number for a song title

_____   2. The correct definition of Adagio

_____   3. Which chapter explores American Indian Music

_____   4. How to spell "concerto"

_____   5. The life story of Brahms

_____   6. Information on the Baroque period in music history

_____   7. If there are any jobs available for a musician

_____   8. The map location of Interlochen National Music Camp in Michigan

_____   9. A list of addresses for all the major recording companies in the USA

_____   10. What's new in music this week

_____   11. The words and music to "Swing Low, Sweet Chariot."

_____   12. Recorded hit songs around the world

BILLBOARD MAGAZINE	TABLE OF CONTENTS	AN AUTOBIOGRAPHY
TIME MAGAZINE	ENCYCLOPEDIA	INDEX OF A SONG BOOK
LOCAL NEWSPAPER	UNITED STATES MAP	GLOSSARY OF A MUSIC BOOK
DICTIONARY	A BOOK ON SPIRITUALS	STANDARD AND POOR'S CORPORATE RECORDS

HOW'S YOUR GEOGRAPHY?   3-25

Imagine you're taking a trip around the country to hear different types of music. Identify the places on the map with the following codes.

(J)   Dixieland Jazz in New Orleans, Louisiana
(B)   Bluegrass Concert in Lexington, Kentucky
(C)   Country-Western in Austin, Texas
(N)   Newport Jazz Festival in Newport, Rhode Island
(L)   New York Philharmonic at Lincoln Center in New York City
(M)   A Broadway musical in New York City
(A)   A performance of *Aida* at the Metropolitan Opera House in New York City
(O)   Grand Ole Opry in Nashville, Tennessee
(I)   Interlochen National Music Camp in Interlochen, Michigan
(F)   Monterey Jazz Festival in Monterey, California
(G)   An off-Broadway musical at the Coconut Grove Playhouse in Miami, Florida
(P)   The Boston Pops in Boston, Massachusetts

FOUR FOR THE SHOW   3-26

Fill in the blanks from the answers at the bottom of the page.

1. Barbershop style is characterized by a balance and blend of ____

   _____ .

2. The barbershop tenor uses little _____

   _____ .

3. When reading barbershop music for women's voices, the treble clef is sung as it is written and the bass clef is transposed an octave

   _____ .

4. To hear the tonic note for a song to be sung, the key note is usually

   blown on the _____ .

5. What distinguishes barbershop harmonization from other vocal

   groups is the _____

   _____ .

6. Barbershop music is usually sung _____ .

7. Rather than the top voice singing the melody as in most other forms of choral music, the

   melody or "lead" in a barbershop arrangement is carried by the _____ .

8. Barbershop arrangements are voiced in such a manner that complete chords are always

   _____ .

9. Lyric sopranos generally make good barbershop _____ .

10. A barbershop chord is composed of four harmonizing _____ .

vibrato	four voices	higher	pitch pipe
voicing of chords	tenors	a cappella	
present	second voice part		tones

Activities for Learning About
MUSICALS

Name _____

Date _____

Score _____

Class _____

WHAT MAKES A MUSICAL?

Do you know what the following plays—*Annie, The Wiz, The Sound of Music, The Music Man,* and *Grease*—have in common?

They are all musicals. You can see a musical on Broadway, at the local children's theatre, or even on television. What are the special qualities that make up a musical? Try to list five characteristics of a musical in the space below. Use the back of this sheet if you can think of more.

CHARACTERISTICS OF A MUSICAL

1. _____

_____

_____

2. _____

_____

3. _____

_____

4. _____

_____

5. _____

_____

_____

MAKE A RESERVATION   3–28

Pretend your family is planning to attend a musical on Broadway. You have been delegated to write a letter to make the reservations. Only seven of the ten items listed below should be included in your letter. Complete the activity by crossing out the three items you will not use.

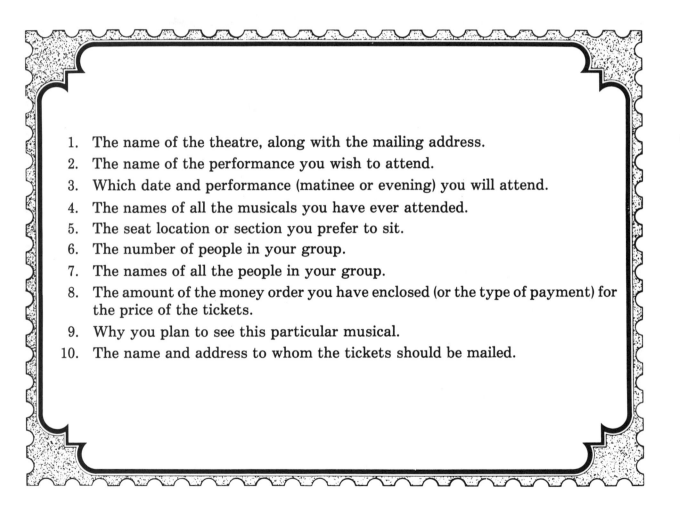

1. The name of the theatre, along with the mailing address.
2. The name of the performance you wish to attend.
3. Which date and performance (matinee or evening) you will attend.
4. The names of all the musicals you have ever attended.
5. The seat location or section you prefer to sit.
6. The number of people in your group.
7. The names of all the people in your group.
8. The amount of the money order you have enclosed (or the type of payment) for the price of the tickets.
9. Why you plan to see this particular musical.
10. The name and address to whom the tickets should be mailed.

WHAT'S THE COUNTERPART?   3–29

Draw a line to connect the two words that spell the name of a musical.

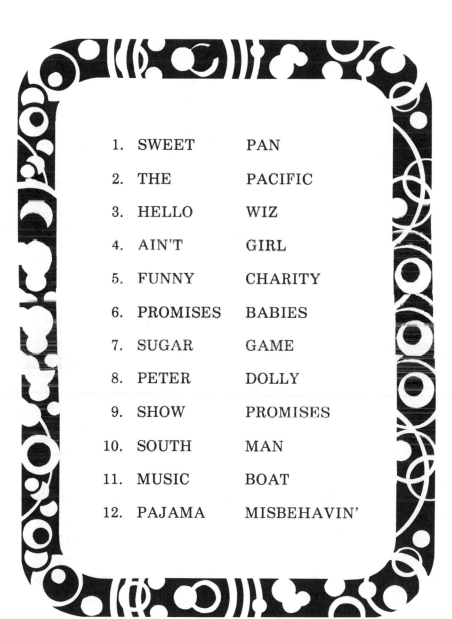

1. SWEET   PAN

2. THE   PACIFIC

3. HELLO   WIZ

4. AIN'T   GIRL

5. FUNNY   CHARITY

6. PROMISES   BABIES

7. SUGAR   GAME

8. PETER   DOLLY

9. SHOW   PROMISES

10. SOUTH   MAN

11. MUSIC   BOAT

12. PAJAMA   MISBEHAVIN'

Name _____   Score _____

Date _____   Class _____

AIM FOR YOUR TARGET   3-30

Win your favorite prize at the carnival by hitting all the targets. Match the song title with the musical by writing the letter in the duck. (If you received a perfect score, draw a picture of the prize you'd like on the back of this paper.)

FUNNY GIRL

FIDDLER
ON THE ROOF

MY FAIR LADY

TITLES OF SONGS:
a. "I Got Plenty of Nothin'"
b. "Summer Nights"
c. "Day by Day"
d. "What I Did for Love"
e. "The Impossible Dream"
f. "People"
g. "Get me to the Church on Time"
h. "Matchmaker"

A CHORUS LINE

GODSPELL

GREASE

PORGY AND BESS

MAN OF
LA MANCHA

Activities for Learning About
OPERA

Name _____   Score _____

Date _____   Class _____

DRAW A SCENE   3–31

Draw a scene from an opera that you watched live, or that you watched on videotape, on television, or heard on some other medium.

Name of opera: _____ **Composer:** _____

OPERA LINGO   3-32

The following musical terms with missing letters are all related to the opera. Find the missing letters by reading the notes above the words. Write the missing letters in the blanks. Then list the terms matching them with their definitions.

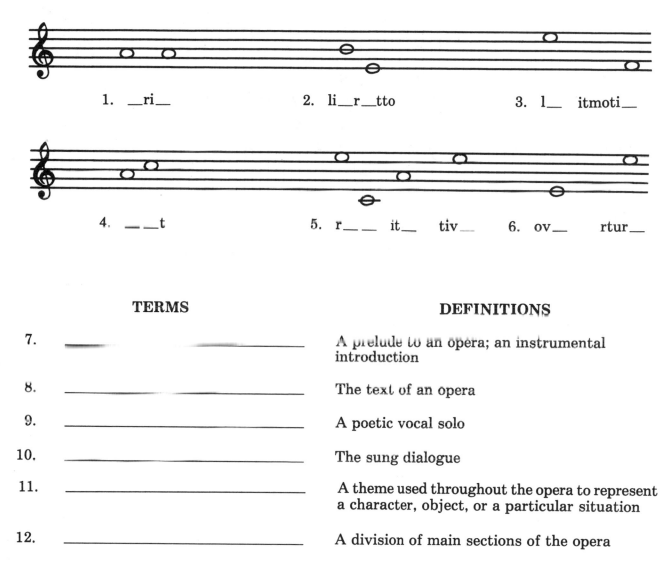

1. __ri__   2. li__r__tto   3. l__ itmoti__

4. __ __t   5. r____ it__ tiv__   6. ov__ rtur__

TERMS	DEFINITIONS
7. _____	A prelude to an opera; an instrumental introduction
8. _____	The text of an opera
9. _____	A poetic vocal solo
10. _____	The sung dialogue
11. _____	A theme used throughout the opera to represent a character, object, or a particular situation
12. _____	A division of main sections of the opera

NOTE KEY:

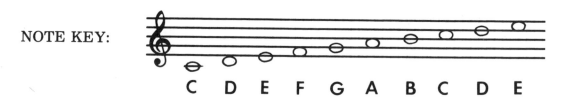

C   D   E   F   G   A   B   C   D   E

Activities for Learning About
POPULAR MUSIC

Name _____   Score _____

Date _____   Class _____

NAME THE HITS   3–33

Think of six songs that have become hits. Write the names of the songs on the records below.

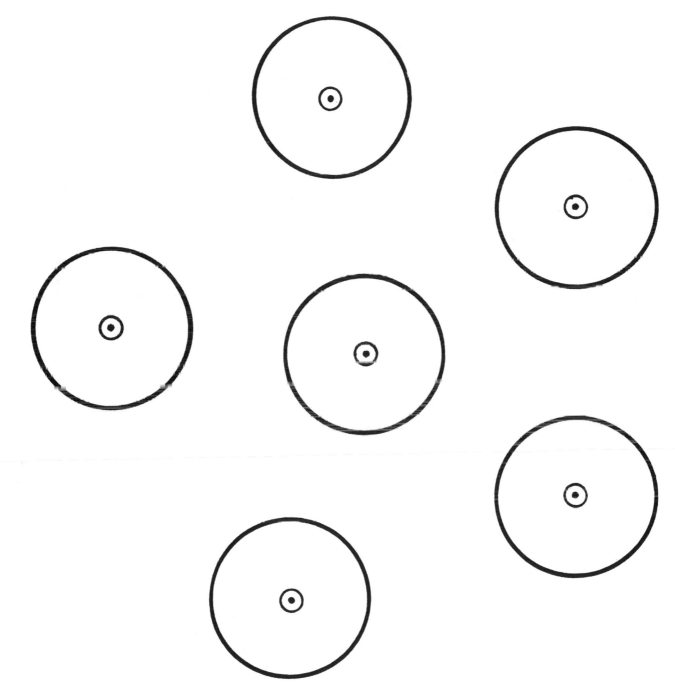

MUSIC OF YESTERDAY, TODAY, AND TOMORROW   3–34

Use the frame below to draw a picture of a popular performing group during one of the following periods in history:

YESTERDAY (before last year); TODAY (right now); TOMORROW (your idea of the future)

The type of dress and instruments should look like those used (or that will be used) during that period. Under your illustration, write the period in history you selected and list at least two different types of popular music performed during that time.

Name _____   Score _____

Date _____   Class _____

PUT THEM IN ORDER   3–35

A music student used a loose-leaf notebook to list popular music from the years 1940 to 1987, allowing one page for each year. In opening the rings of the notebook, the pages fell out. While putting the notebook back in order, it was found that some pages lacked their year reference. These pages are shown below. Write the year reference at the top of each sheet so you can help the music student put them back in place. The years are:

1945 1956 1967 1975 1987

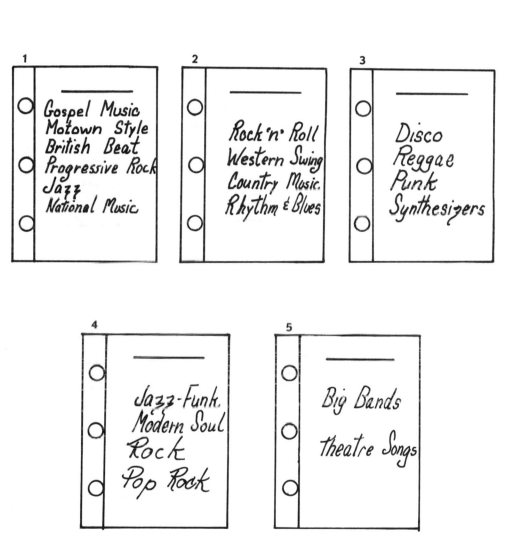

1
Gospel Music
Motown Style
British Beat
Progressive Rock
Jazz
National Music

2
Rock 'n' Roll
Western Swing
Country Music
Rhythm & Blues

3
Disco
Reggae
Punk
Synthesizers

4
Jazz-Funk
Modern Soul
Rock
Pop Rock

5
Big Bands
Theatre Songs

WHEN WERE THEY POPULAR?   3-36

When did these groups of performers first become popular? Write the decade by each group.

1940s   1950s   1960s   1970s   1980s

1. _____   Tommy Dorsey Band
                       Jimmy Dorsey Band
                       Frank Sinatra

2. _____   Michael Jackson
                       Sandi Patti
                       Duran Duran

3. _____   The Beatles
                       Supremes
                       Beach Boys

4. _____   Olivia Newton-John
                       Fleetwood Mac
                       Elton John

5. _____   Johnny Ray
                       Elvis Presley
                       Peggy Lee

Activities for Learning About
PUZZLES

WINDING PATH PUZZLE   3-37

Have you ever gone around and around to get somewhere? In this puzzle that is what you will do. To reach the middle, fill in the blocks with the words suggested by the clues. The last letter of the first word is the first letter of the second word, and so on. After you finish, color in the star.

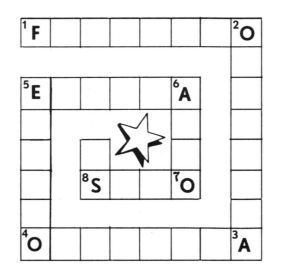

1. A lively Spanish dance
2. Title of a popular musical; the name of a state
3. When the notes of a chord are played in succession
4. The name of a Country song, "___ Blossom Special," by Ervin T. Rosse
5. Another name for Beethoven's Symphony No. 3 in E-flat major
6. The lowest female voice
7. A method to number compositions in the order which they are written
8. Abbreviation for "Sforzando"

Name _____   Score _____

Date _____   Class _____

EXPLORING THE UNKNOWN   3–38

Have you ever explored a new area looking at different sights? Pretend that you will do that today. Start at 1 and follow the path to the end where you see the bus. Do this by filling in the blocks. The last letter of the first word is the first letter of the next word, and so on. Number 14 is done for you.

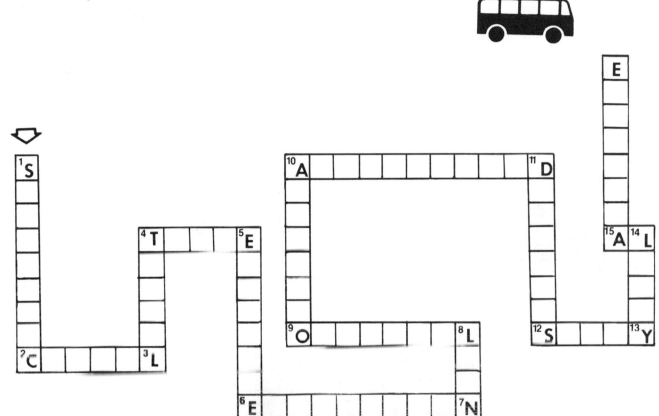

1. Another name for orchestral music
2. Music sung by a choir or chorus
3. A composition of a sad or mournful character (short for lamentation)
4. Ternary form music is divided into ____ parts
5. A piece for several performers
6. The first section of a large musical composition which states the main theme
7. A Christmas song; a French word meaning "tidings"
8. The words of an opera
9. A little opera
10. The opposite of a cappella
11. Contrasting degrees of intensity
12. A composition in the style of an exercise
13. How the Swiss mountaineers sing
14. An Italian word meaning half a string group; "__ __ Meta"
15. Listeners at a concert

THE PERFORMER PUZZLE   3-39

To help you solve this puzzle, the letters are given where the words link together.

ACROSS

  2. Eight singers or players
  6. A set of instrumental compositions
  7. A song such as "Three Blind Mice"
  9. Three singers or players
  10. A tune played or sung by one person
  12. (It.) Quick
  14. A combination of performers
  16. A short, simple instrumental piece
  18. Five performers
  19. An Italian word meaning "slow"

DOWN

  1. Two singers or players
  3. A song of joy or praise
  4. Four singers or players
  5. An Italian word meaning soft
  8. A composition for nine instruments
  10. An extended composition for orchestra
  11. A play set entirely to music
  13. A musical sound
  15. A musical composition given an identifying number
  17. A melody

Activity for Learning About
PUZZLES

3-40   MAKE A MATCH

MAKE A MATCH   3-40

Below are the descriptions of seven different types of sacred music. Finish writing the type by its description. Every other letter for each word in the answer is missing. The missing letters are scrambled in order at the bottom of the page.

1. A hymn tune or sacred tune is called a c__ o __a__e.
2. The celebration of the Eucharist of the Last Supper, including the Kyrie, the Gloria, the Credo, the Sanctus and the Agnus Dei, is called the m__s__.
3. The earliest form of music in the Christian church, a liturgical chant, is called a G__e__o__i__n C__a__t.
4. A musical introduction is called a p__e__u__e.
5. An old form of church music, all notes of equal value and unison singing is called p__a__ns__n__.
6. A story or play set to music for chorus and instrumental accompaniment is called a c__n__a__a
7. The *St. Matthew Passion* by J.S. Bach uses a theme from the Bible with music written for solo voices, chorus, and orchestra. It is called an o__a__o__i__.

The letters for each answer are in mixed order:
1. lhr   2. sa   3. grar hn   4. rdl   5. ilgo
6. att   7. ortr

Activity for Learning About
SPIRITUALS

3-41   WRITE THE LYRICS

Name _____

Date _____

Score _____

Class _____

WRITE THE LYRICS

3-41

Below are the titles and beginning measures of five well-known spirituals. Finish the examples by writing the lyrics (words) under each staff. The first two measures of "We Shall Overcome" are done for you.

1. **We Shall Overcome**

We shall o-ver-come ___

2. **He's Got the Whole World in His Hands**

3. **Michael, Row the Boat Ashore**

4. **Nobody Knows the Trouble I've Seen**

5. **Swing Low, Sweet Chariot**

Activities for Learning About
SYMPHONIC FORMS

CONCERTO CLUES   3-42

Use this code to identify the words that finish the sentences below about the concerto form.

A	B	C	D	E	F	G	H	I	J	K	L	M
1	2	3	4	5	6	7	8	9	10	11	12	13

N	O	P	Q	R	S	T	U	V	W	X	Y	Z
14	15	16	17	18	19	20	21	22	23	24	25	26

1. Since the mid-eighteenth century there have generally been three movements in the
   __ __ __ __ __ __ __ __.
   3 15 14 3 5 18 20 15

2. A concerto is written for a solo instrument and __ __ __ __ __ __ __ __ __.
   15 18 3 8 5 19 20 18 1

3. The first movement of a concerto is in sonata __ __ __ __.
   6 15 18 13

4. The second movement is __ __ __ __.
   19 12 15 23

5. The final movement is in sonata form or __ __ __ __ __ form.
   18 15 14 4 15

6. Rondo form is characterized by the main theme being repeated after each new theme is
   __ __ __ __ __ __ __ __ __ __.
   9 14 20 18 15 4 21 3 5 4

7. The concerto was an outgrowth of the concerto grosso form with three movements for
   a group of three soloists and __ __ __ __ __ __ __ __ __ __ __ __ __ __.
   1 3 3 15 13 16 1 14 9 13 5 14 20

8. One of the earliest composers of the concerto grosso form was Arcangelo
   __ __ __ __ __ __ __.
   3 15 18 5 12 12 9

MATCH THE DATES 3-43

Listed below are the dates for different periods in music history. Each period is known by a name. Write the names opposite the dates. Each space stands for a letter. Then check your answers with the puzzle square, beginning where the baton is pointing and moving down.

800–1650	_ _ _ _ _ _ _ _ _ _
1650–1750	_ _ _ _ _ _ _ _
1750–1820	_ _ _ _ _ _ _ _ _ _
1820–1900	_ _ _ _ _ _ _ _ _
1900–Present	_ _ _ _ _ _ _ _ _ _ _

SPELL IT WITH NOTES

3-44

Below are the names of different types of music. Each name has missing letters. Find the letters by reading the notes above the words. Complete the words by writing the letter names on the blanks. Then write the types of music in the same order on the blanks below to match their definitions.

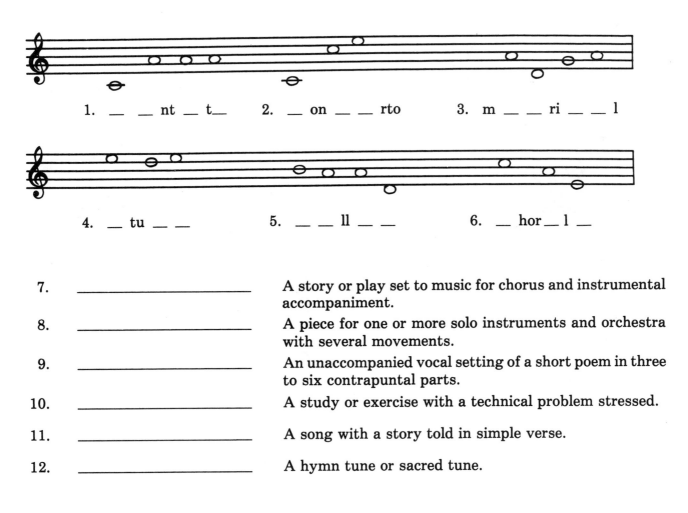

1. _ _ nt _ t_   2. _ on _ _ rto   3. m _ _ ri _ _ l

4. _ tu _ _   5. _ _ ll _ _   6. _ hor _ l _

7. _____ A story or play set to music for chorus and instrumental accompaniment.

8. _____ A piece for one or more solo instruments and orchestra with several movements.

9. _____ An unaccompanied vocal setting of a short poem in three to six contrapuntal parts.

10. _____ A study or exercise with a technical problem stressed.

11. _____ A song with a story told in simple verse.

12. _____ A hymn tune or sacred tune.

NOTE KEY:

C D E F G A B C D E

UNSCRAMBLE AND MATCH   3–45

See how many of the symphonic forms you can identify by reading the definitions. Then check your answers with the words written in mirror code at the bottom of the page.

a. S _____ • A work usually in four movements—Allegro, Adagio, Scherzo, and Allegro.

b. S _____ P _____ • Also called a tone poem; a one-movement composition using a free form.

c. O _____ • An instrumental prelude to introduce an opera.

d. N _____ • A composition for one or more solo performers and orchestra, usually in three movements.

e. P _____ M _____ • A symphony describing nonmusical ideas.

f. I _____ M _____ • Music to be played during a play, as background music, or between acts.

g. B _____ M _____ • A composition, usually in the form of a suite, intended to accompany a ballet.

h. S _____ V _____ • A work for orchestra in theme-and-variation form.

i. S _____ S _____ • A work with several movements and no standard structure.

_____

List the decoded words in order.

1. _____

2. _____   SYMPHONY

3. _____   SYMPHONIC POEM

4. _____   OVERTURE

5. _____   NOCTURNE

6. _____   PROGRAM MUSIC

7. _____   INCIDENTAL MUSIC

8. _____   BALLET MUSIC

9. _____   SYMPHONIC VARIATION

                                 SYMPHONIC SUITE

FINISH THE CANON

3-46

A CANON is a composition for two or more voice parts using imitation.

Use the Note Key to write the letter names of notes of both the bass and treble staffs in the song below. Then finish writing the canon on the treble staff using the same notes as the melody in the bass staff. The first and last measures of the treble staff are done for you. The arrows are drawn to show you how the bass melody is identical to the treble melody, but instead of sounding together, it is two beats behind (like an echo).

NOTE
KEY

D E F G A   D E F G A

CANON I

Moderato

Konrad Max Kunz
(1812–1875)

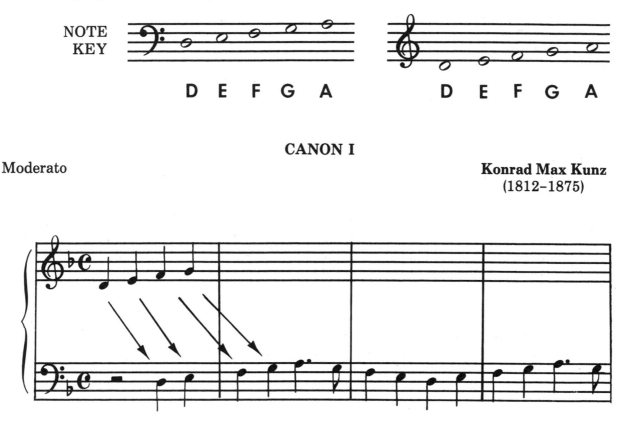

Name _____   Score _____

Date _____   Class _____

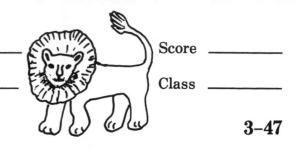

TACKLE THE TITLE   3-47

PROGRAM MUSIC or PROGRAMME MUSIC is a term for instrumental music that tells a story or describes a specific situation.

Below are descriptions of five different compositions that can be classified as program music. Choose a title for each of them from the list at the bottom of the page. Write your answers on the blanks.

The composer for this tone poem was inspired by a prankster in an old German legend. There are two main themes that appear throughout the work. The French horn theme describes this character's mischievous nature. The clarinet describes the person himself.

1. _____

The various sections of this suite represent different paintings as seen through the eyes of a composer. One section entitled, "The Ballet of the Unhatched Chicks" sounds like little chickens moving in their shells.

2. _____

A girl dreams that the Christmas present she received is really a handsome prince. After leading the toys into battle against the mice, the prince takes the girl to Arabia where she is greeted by the Sugarplum Fairy. There is entertainment with games, dances, and toys.

3. _____

A magician has a secret way of getting his broom to do as he commands. The magician's apprentice imitates his directions and the broom becomes animated. But, the apprentice doesn't know how to stop the broom.

4. _____

This is a suite for two pianos and orchestra that characterizes various animals. It begins with the "Introduction and Royal March of the Lion" and ends with the "Finale" where all the characters return to take a final bow.

5. _____

Pictures at an Exhibition	*Carnival of the Animals*	*Till Eulenspiegel*
The Sorcerer's Apprentice		*Nutcracker* Suite

© 1987 by Parker Publishing Company, Inc.

Name _____   Score _____

Date _____   Class _____

SONATA-ALLEGRO FORM WORD SEARCH   3–48

Use these words—REPLICA, VARIED, THEMES, THREE, COMPOSITION, SONATA, FORM, PIECE, CENTURY, SYMPHONY, PARTS, REPEAT—to complete the sentences about Sonata-Allegro Form. Then find these words in the word search and circle them. The words can be found horizontally and vertically.

1. Sonata actually means "sound _ _ _ _ _."

2. The sonata is one of the highest developments of musical _ _ _ _.

3. Another name for Sonata-Allegro Form is _ _ _ _ _ _ Form.

4. The sonata form developed in the eighteenth _ _ _ _ _ _ _.

5. The sonata form can usually be found in the first movements of a concerto, sonata, string quartet and _ _ _ _ _ _ _ _.

6. When we talk about the sonata as having ternary form, we mean it has _ _ _ _ _ distinct parts.

7. A typical sonata is an instrumental _ _ _ _ _ _ _ _ _ _ _.

8. The three _ _ _ _ _ of a sonata are known as the exposition, development and recapitulation.

9. In the exposition, two principal _ _ _ _ _ _ are stated.

10. In the development the themes are enlarged and _ _ _ _ _ _ _.

11. Recapitulation means to _ _ _ _ _ _ the themes as they appear in the exposition.

12. A Sonatina (little sonata) is a modified _ _ _ _ _ _ _ of the Sonata-Allegro form.

```
M C E C X V A E F
X P S O N A T A E
P A S M L R Z I E
J R E P L I C A N
O T W O Q E E N B
I S C S E D N A T
R I L I T O T S U
M S A T T M U Y K
A R U I H D R M R
E E F O R M Y P D
A P F N E I R H T
I E P I E C E O B
D A E M F T U N I
U T H E M E S Y E
Y A D G E T X Y X
```

Name _____   Score _____

Date _____   Class _____

ANALYZE THE FORM   3–49

One of the simplest forms in music is A B A FORM or THREE-PART SONG FORM. In this form there is a main theme, a contrasting section called the recapitulation, and the repetition of the main section (A B A), also as (A A B A).

"The Marines' Hymn" is in THREE-PART SONG FORM. Use the key below as your guide to analyze where each new phrase begins and ends. Write the correct letter above the staff for the beginning of the first note of each new section of music.

KEY:
A = The first complete musical phrase
A = Repeat of the first phrase
B = Contrasting phrase
A = Repeat of the original statement

THE MARINES' HYMN

From the halls of Mon-te-zu-ma, To the shores of Trip-o-li, We will

fight our coun-try's bat-tles, On the land and on the sea. First to

fight for right and free-dom, And to keep our hon-or clean, We are

proud to claim the ti-tle of U-nit-ed States Ma-rines.

MAKING ALPHABET SOUP

The following groups of titles represent five forms of music which are named in the bowls of alphabet soup. Match the groups of titles with their forms by writing their identifying letters in the bowls. Be sure you print the letters in their listed orders. When you are finished, your answers will spell out a message.

(D) *Pathetique* by Tchaikovsky
(I) The *Toy* Symphony by Haydn
(D) *Eroica* by Beethoven

(N) Overture to *A Midsummer Night's Dream* by Mendelssohn
(O) Overture to *The Barber of Seville* by Rossini
(W) Overture to *Don Giovanni* by Mozart

(W) *The Sorcerer's Apprentice* by Dukas
(O) *Till Eulenspiegel* by Richard Strauss
(R) *Danse Macabre* by Saint-Saëns
(K) *The Moldau* by Smetana

(Y) *Hansel and Gretel* by Humperdinck
(O) *Amahl and the Night Visitors* by Menotti
(U) *Carmen* by Bizet

(T) *Death Valley* Suite by Grofé
(H) *Scheherazade* by Rimsky-Korsakov
(E) *Peer Gynt* Suite by Grieg

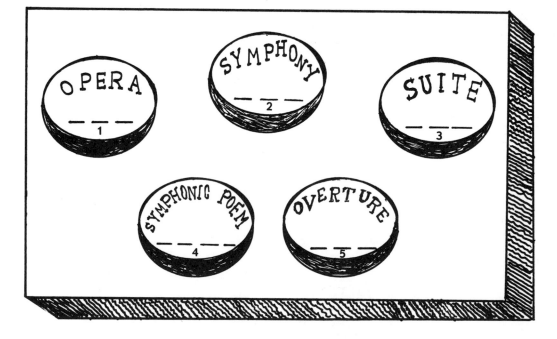

Answer Key for
Types of Musical Form and Composition

3-1 INTEREST INVENTORY

Answers will vary.

3-2 QUESTIONS FROM THE SITTER

1.	a	5.	a	9.	b
2.	c	6.	a	10.	b
3.	c	7.	c	11.	c
4.	b	8.	c	12.	a

3-3 WHAT DO YOU HEAR?

Answers will vary.

3-4 CLASSIFY THE SOUNDS

Answers will vary.

3-5 WHAT'S THAT SOUND?

Answers will vary.

3-6 ENTER THE SINGING GAME CONTEST

Answers will vary.

3-7 A DISNEY QUIZ

1. *Mary Poppins*
2. *Jungle Book*
3. *Cinderella*
4. *Peter Pan*
5. *Westward Ho the Wagons*
6. *Babes in Toyland*
7. *Lady and the Tramp*
8. *Alice in Wonderland*

3-8 THE COUNTRY SCRAMBLE

1. COUNTRY WESTERN
2. GUITAR
3. COUNTRY
4. NASHVILLE, TENNESSEE
5. ROY ACUFF
6. BANJO
7. Answers will vary.
8. GRAND OLD OPRY
9. BLUEGRASS
10. BILL MONROE

3-9 IDENTIFY THE COWBOY SONGS

1. "Red River Valley"
2. "Git Along, Little Dogies"
3. "Home on the Range"
4. "My Home's in Montana"
5. "The Streets of Laredo"

3-10 JUST DAYDREAMING

Pictures will vary.

3-11 YOU DRAW IT

Pictures will vary.

3-12 MY FAVORITE TYPE OF MUSIC IS . . .

Answers will vary.

3-13 WRITE A COVER STORY

Answers will vary.

3-14 YOU'RE THE CRITIC

Answers will vary.

3-15 DIAL A DANCE

1. Polka
2. Mazurka
3. Tarantella
4. Waltz

5. Bolero
6. Habañera
7. Tango
8. Disco

3-16 DABBLING IN DANCE

3-17 FINISH THE TITLES

1. MOUNTAIN
2. GALS
3. RHODY
4. VALLEY

5. DRILL
6. HENRY
7. AGO
8. PINS

9. ME
10. PIKE

3-18 WHAT'S NEXT?

1. c
2. b
3. e
4. a
5. d

3-19 RIFFS, LICKS, AND CHOPS

This is a self-checking activity. Before introducing this activity, familiarize your students with the terms used through a variety of listening experiences.

3-20 DECODE THE NICKNAMES

Note Names: C D E F G A B C

1. Cannonball
2. Satchmo
3. Buddy
4. Baby
5. Fatha
6. Lightnin'
7. Leadbelly
8. Jelly
9. Fats
10. Bird
11. Ma
12. Fats

3-21 WHICH TYPE IS IT?

a. R
b. S
c. C
d. P

3-22 MARCH TO THE LIBRARY

Marches are generally written in $\frac{2}{4}$, $\frac{4}{4}$, or $\frac{6}{8}$ time. The different sections or parts generally found in a march are the minuet with trio. This three-part song form is called ABA form. Some of John Philip Sousa's famous marches are "The Stars and Stripes Forever," "Semper Fidelis," "El Capitan," "The Thunderer," "The Washington Post," and "The Black Horse Troop." Other popular marches are "Seventy-Six Trombones" by Meredith Willson and "March Militaire" by Franz Schubert.

1. The word "march" means music designed to be played for marching. Marches are always in simple rhythm and regular phrases.
2. Parades, military band concerts, circuses, concert halls, theaters
3. John Philip Sousa, "March King"
4. Over 100 marches (Sousa wrote exactly 136 marches)
5. Answers will vary.
6. Answers will vary.

3-23 LEARNING OUR NATIONAL ANTHEM

This activity is designed to be used as a research project.

1. c
2. a
3. c, b, c, a
4. b
5. b
6. c
7. a
8. a
9. c
10. a

11. Suggested answers: stand, place hand over heart, face the flag, sing the national anthem

12. Francis Scott Key wrote the words to our national anthem in 1814 when England and the United States were at war. He had boarded a British warship, along with another American, in an attempt to free an American prisoner. The two men were held on board ship overnight, long enough for the British to carry out their plans to destroy Fort McHenry. While Key knew the fort was in jeopardy, he watched the shore carefully all night to observe what was happening. Just after dawn, Key saw the American flag and he was elated. It was at that moment that he quickly wrote some poetry on an envelope. Later, it was suggested that the poem be set to the music of the old English tune "To Anacreon in Heaven."

3–24   FIND THE RESOURCE

1. Index of a song book
2. Glossary of a music book
3. Table of contents
4. Dictionary
5. An autobiography
6. Encyclopedia
7. Local newspaper
8. United States map
9. *Standard and Poor's Corporation Records*
10. *Time* Magazine
11. A book on spirituals
12. *Billboard Magazine*

3–25   HOW'S YOUR GEOGRAPHY?

3–26   FOUR FOR THE SHOW

1. four voices
2. vibrato
3. higher
4. pitch pipe
5. voicing of chords
6. a cappella
7. second voice part
8. present
9. tenors
10. tones

3–27   WHAT MAKES A MUSICAL?

Answers will vary. Suggested answers are:

1. A musical is a form of entertainment for the stage.
2. Successful musicals are performed on Broadway.

3. A musical is a combination of spoken dialogue, songs, and orchestral music.

4. A musical usually centers around an all-American theme.

5. The story is an integral part of the songs and dance.

6. Successful musicals travel by road shows to all parts of the country (and world).

7. A musical has a plot.

8. The musical is an outgrowth of the minstrel show, variety shows, and operettas.

3-28 MAKE A RESERVATION

Items to cross out: 4, 7, 9

Prior to completing this activity, make students aware of local musical productions being advertised in the newspaper. Ask students to bring advertisements from any newspaper to class, showing the time and date of a performance. Have students check for ticket prices, seat locations, and any other helpful information. As a class project, try writing a sample letter on the chalkboard to make reservations.

3-29 WHAT'S THE COUNTERPART?

1. SWEET CHARITY
2. THE WIZ
3. HELLO DOLLY
4. AIN'T MISBEHAVIN'
5. FUNNY GIRL
6. PROMISES, PROMISES
7. SUGAR BABIES
8. PETER PAN
9. SHOW BOAT
10. SOUTH PACIFIC
11. MUSIC MAN
12. PAJAMA GAME

3-30 AIM FOR YOUR TARGET

FIDDLER ON THE ROOF—h

FUNNY GIRL f

MY FAIR LADY g

GODSPELL—c

MAN OF LA MANCHA—e

PORGY AND BESS—a

GREASE—b

A CHORUS LINE—d

3-31 DRAW A SCENE

Pictures will vary.

3-32 OPERA LINGO

1. aria
2. libretto
3. leitmotif
4. act
5. recitative
6. overture
7. overture
8. libretto
9. aria
10. recitative
11. leitmotif
12. act

3-33 NAME THE HITS

Answers will vary.

3-34 MUSIC OF YESTERDAY, TODAY, AND TOMORROW

You might suggest that "yesterday" be ten years ago; "future," ten years from now. Pictures will vary.

3-35 PUT THEM IN ORDER

1. 1967
2. 1956
3. 1975

4. 1987
5. 1945

3-36 WHEN WERE THEY POPULAR?

1. 1940s
2. 1980s
3. 1960s

4. 1970s
5. 1950s

3-37 WINDING PATH PUZZLE

3-38 EXPLORING THE UNKNOWN

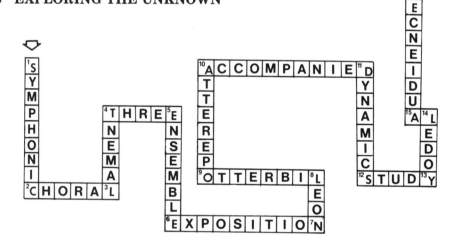

3-39 THE PERFORMER PUZZLE

Answer Key for *Types of Musical Form and Composition* 73

3-40 MAKE A MATCH

1. chorale
2. mass
3. Gregorian chant
4. prelude

5. plainsong
6. cantata
7. oratorio

3-41 WRITE THE LYRICS

1. We Shall Overcome

We shall ov-er-come,____ We shall ov-er ——— come ____

2. He's Got the Whole World in His Hands

He's got the whole world__ in his hands,_He's got the

3. Michael, Row the Boat Ashore

Mi—chael, row the boat a—shore, Hal le—lu—jah, Mi-chael,

4. Nobody Knows the Trouble I've Seen

No—bo—dy knows the trou-ble I've seen, No—bo—dy knows but

5. Swing Low, Sweet Chariot

Swing low sweet cha—ri—ot,___ com-in' for to car-ry me home

3-42 CONCERTO CLUES

This activity is self-checking.

1. CONCERTO
2. ORCHESTRA
3. FORM

4. SLOW
5. RONDO
6. INTRODUCED

7. ACCOMPANIMENT
8. CORELLI

3-43 MATCH THE DATES

This activity is self-checking.

800–1650:	Polyphonic
1650–1750:	Baroque
1750–1820:	Classical
1820–1900:	Romantic
1900–Present:	Scientific

3-44   SPELL IT WITH NOTES

This activity is self-checking.

1. cantata
2. concerto
3. madrigal
4. etude
5. ballad
6. chorale

7. cantata
8. concerto
9. madrigal
10. etude
11. ballad
12. chorale

3-45   UNSCRAMBLE AND MATCH

This activity is self-checking.

a. SYMPHONY
b. SYMPHONIC POEM
c. OVERTURE
d. NOCTURNE
e. PROGRAM MUSIC

f. INCIDENTAL MUSIC
g. BALLET MUSIC
h. SYMPHONIC VARIATION
i. SYMPHONIC SUITE

3-46   FINISH THE CANON

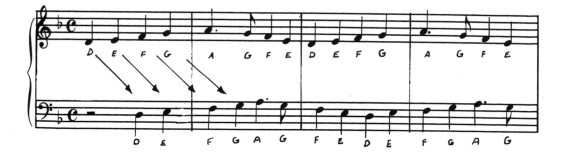

3-47   TACKLE THE TITLE

1. *Till Eulenspiegel*
2. *Pictures at an Exhibition*
3. *Nutcracker* Suite

4. *The Sorcerer's Apprentice*
5. *Carnival of the Animals*

3-48 SONATA-ALLEGRO FORM WORD SEARCH

1. PIECE
2. FORM
3. SONATA
4. CENTURY
5. SYMPHONY
6. THREE
7. COMPOSITION
8. PARTS
9. THEMES
10. VARIED
11. REPEAT
12. REPLICA

```
M C E C X V A E F
X P S O N A T A E
P A S M L R Z I E
J R E P L I C A N
O T W O Q E E N B
I S C S E D N A T
R I L I T O T S U
M S A T M U Y K
A R U I H D R M R
E E F O R M Y P D
A P F N E I R H T
I E P I E C E O B
D A E M F T U N I
U T H E M E S Y E
Y A D G E T X Y X
```

3-49 ANALYZE THE FORM

• "A" should be written above the word "From," the first word of the song.
• "A" should be written above the word "We," located at the end of the first staff.
• "B" should be written above the word "First," located at the end of the second staff.
• "A" should be written above the word "We," located at the end of the third staff.

3-50 MAKING ALPHABET SOUP

1. YOU
2. DID
3. THE
4. WORK
5. NOW

Progress Chart for
Types of Musical Form and Composition

Use this chart to keep a record of activities completed for each class. List your classes (or students) in the given spaces at the right. As each activity is completed for a class, mark an "X" in the appropriate column.

Activity Number/Title	Skill Involved				
Children's Music					
3-1 INTEREST INVENTORY	Taking a personal assessment to determine own favorite type of music				
3-2 QUESTIONS FROM THE SITTER	Recalling facts about nursery songs				
3-3 WHAT DO YOU HEAR?	Listing and classifying indoor sounds according to loud and soft				
3-4 CLASSIFY THE SOUNDS	Listing and classifying outdoor sounds according to loud and soft				
3-5 WHAT'S THAT SOUND?	Classifying country and city sounds by types, origins, and descriptions				
3-6 ENTER THE SINGING GAME CONTEST	Creating a musical game				
3-7 A DISNEY QUIZ	Matching Disney songs with productions				
Country-Western					
3-8 THE COUNTRY SCRAMBLE	Recalling facts about country music				
Cowboy Songs					
3-9 IDENTIFY THE COWBOY SONGS	Matching titles of cowboy songs with beginning words and notes				
Creative Drawing					
3-10 JUST DAYDREAMING	Drawing a picture of one's favorite type of music				
3-11 YOU DRAW IT	Sketching a picture of a type of music				

Activity Number/Title	Skill Involved	

Creative Writing

3-12	MY FAVORITE TYPE OF MUSIC IS . . .	Writing a paragraph about one's favorite type of music
3-13	WRITE A COVER STORY	Writing an article about an upcoming musical event
3-14	YOU'RE THE CRITIC	Writing a review of a musical event

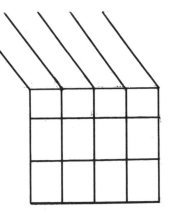

Dance

3-15	DIAL A DANCE	Identifying names of national dances
3-16	DABBLING IN DANCE	Recalling facts about various dances

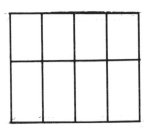

Folk Songs

3-17	FINISH THE TITLES	Completing the last word in the titles of American folk songs
3-18	WHAT'S NEXT?	Drawing in the missing note at the end of a musical example

Jazz

3-19	RIFFS, LICKS, AND CHOPS	Studying jazz terminology
3-20	DECODE THE NICKNAMES	Writing nicknames of famous jazz musicians using a note code

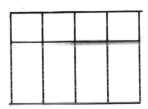

Library Research

3-21	WHICH TYPE IS IT?	Classifying patriotic songs, spirituals, rounds, sea songs, and chanties
3-22	MARCH TO THE LIBRARY	Researching marches
3-23	LEARNING OUR NATIONAL ANTHEM	Analyzing "The Star-Spangled Banner"
3-24	FIND THE RESOURCE	Matching types of resources with types of information needed
3-25	HOW'S YOUR GEOGRAPHY?	Identifying places on the map to indicate where certain musical events are held
3-26	FOUR FOR THE SHOW	Examining characteristics of barbershop music

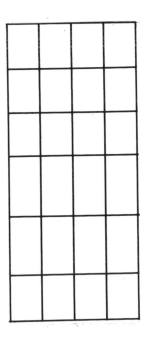

Activity Number/Title		Skill Involved	

Musicals

3–27	WHAT MAKES A MUSICAL?	Listing five characteristics of a musical	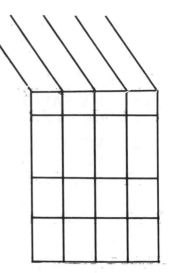
3–28	MAKE A RESERVATION	Deciding criterion to make reservations for a musical on Broadway	
3–29	WHAT'S THE COUNTERPART?	Matching two words that spell the name of a musical	
3–30	AIM FOR YOUR TARGET	Matching song titles with musicals	

Opera

| 3–31 | DRAW A SCENE | Drawing a scene from a favorite opera |  |
| 3–32 | OPERA LINGO | Using a note code to spell opera terms and matching terms with definitions | |

Popular Music

3–33	NAME THE HITS	Naming hit records of current popular performers	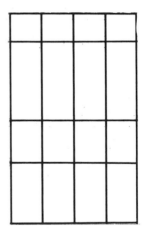
3–34	MUSIC OF YESTERDAY, TODAY, AND TOMORROW	Illustrating performing groups of various periods and listing pop music of the time	
3–35	PUT THEM IN ORDER	Classifying popular music according to dates	
3–36	WHEN WERE THEY POPULAR?	Writing the decade for when the performing group was popular	

Puzzles

3–37	WINDING PATH PUZZLE	Completing a puzzle on music terminology and musical forms using sentence clues	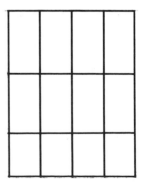
3–38	EXPLORING THE UNKNOWN	Solving a puzzle using sentence clues including music terminology and forms	
3–39	THE PERFORMER PUZZLE	Recalling facts about musical forms and terminology	

Religious (Sacred) Music

| 3–40 | MAKE A MATCH | Identifying various forms of sacred music and matching with definitions | 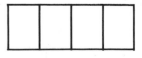 |

Activity Number/Title	Skill Involved	

Spirituals

3-41	WRITE THE LYRICS	Writing the lyrics for beginning bars of five well-known spirituals

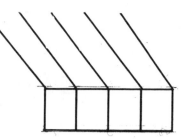

Symphonic Forms

3-42	CONCERTO CLUES	Using a code to identify terms relating to a concerto
3-43	MATCH THE DATES	Using a puzzle square to match dates with periods in history
3-44	SPELL IT WITH NOTES	Naming various forms of music using a note code and matching it with definitions
3-45	UNSCRAMBLE AND MATCH	Unscrambling names of symphonic forms to match definitions
3-46	FINISH THE CANON	Finishing a canon using notation on a treble staff
3-47	TACKLE THE TITLE	Matching descriptions of program music with titles
3-48	SONATA-ALLEGRO FORM WORD SEARCH	Completing sentences about sonata-allegro form
3 10	ANALYZE THE FORM	Analyzing "The Marines' Hymn" as Three-Part Song Form (AABA)
3-50	MAKING ALPHABET SOUP	Classifying various forms of composition

Types of Musical Composition and Form

ABA Form	madrigal
a cappella	march
accompanied	musical
aria	opera
ballad	operetta
ballet	orchestral
ballroom music	overture
band	pitch
barbershop quartet	popular
bluegrass	program music
canon	recitative
cantata	religious
chanties	rhythm
choir	rock
chorale	rondo
chorus	round
concerto	sacred
concerto grosso	sea song
country/country western	sonata
cowboy songs	sonata-allegro
dynamics	sonatina
etude	spiritual
folk	suite
form	symphonic poem
improvisation	symphony
incidental music	tempo
jazz	theme
libretto	timbre
lyrics	volume

Name _____

Date _____

Craft Project for *Types of Musical Form and Composition*

MINI BOOKLET

Objective: The Mini Booklet is designed to bring out meaningful relationships and concepts in the area of musical form and types of music. The booklet will add incentive for additional learning and will encourage students to develop generalizations in this specific area of music education. It will also add interest in independent study and will encourage the use of encyclopedias and other reference material.

Materials Needed:

- 9" × 12" color construction paper
- Several sheets of plain 8½" × 11" paper
- Hole puncher
- Two pieces of colored yarn
- Scissors
- *Optional:* Copies of the cover design pattern
- *Optional:* Paste
- *Optional:* Markers

Construction Directions:

1. Cut the construction paper in half to form two 4½" × 6" covers. Cut out the cover design pattern, center it and paste it on the front cover of the booklet; or create your own design on the construction paper with markers.

2. Fold or cut in half several sheets of plain paper to make as many 4¼" × 5½" sheets as you need.

3. With a hole puncher, punch two holes along the left side of each page and the covers. Make sure the holes are all in the same place on every sheet.

4. Line up all the pages inside the covers. Thread a piece of colored yarn through each set of holes, and tie the loose ends in a bow.

Try creating your own original cover design!

Uses:

1. Include interesting facts learned about a particular type of music, such as in what part of the world it originated, and paste newspaper or magazine pictures.

2. Write several short paragraphs describing a certain form or type of music. Mention in what period of history it became popular, list musical examples, mention composers, who listens to the music, instruments typically used, and so on.

3. Find information on musical forms in at least two sources. Check encyclopedias, library books, filmstrips, music dictionary, and/or music series books. List the bibliography.

4. Read and collect information in note form. Rewrite the facts in the mini booklet using good sentence structure. Check for spelling and grammatical errors.

5. Use the mini booklets as a discovery project. Have the students write about their own choice of music type or form without naming it. Then, upon completion, ask the students to exchange the booklets to determine by the clues what form or type of music the author was researching.

Name _____

Date _____

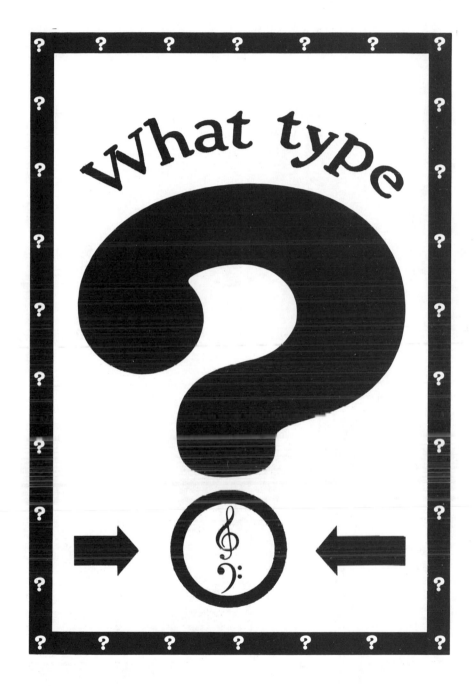

Incentive Badges

To the teacher: Cut apart badges and keep in a handy 3″ × 5″ file box along with tape. Encourage students to write their names and the date on the backs of their badges and to wear them.

Good Listener

MUSIC AWARD

A Pledge

DO IT NOW!

_____
_____
_____
(name)

MUSIC TOKEN

MUSIC AWARD

THANKS

BEST BEHAVIOR

"Busy as a bee"

MUSIC AWARD

CERTIFICATE

TO: FOR:

DOUBLE EXTRA BONUS
MUSIC AWARD
NAME _____
_____

WITH THIS COUPON...
NAME _____
IS ENTITLED TO _____
_____
MUSIC AWARD

For hopping to it!
Good helper badge
in music class.

Watch Out!

Best in the class . . .
MUSIC AWARD

Creative WRITING

MUSIC CLASS AWARD

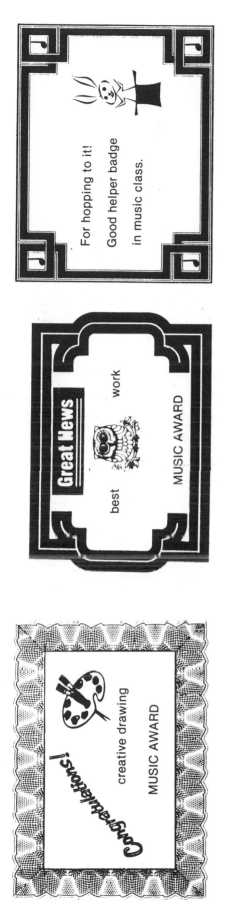

Great News

best   work

MUSIC AWARD

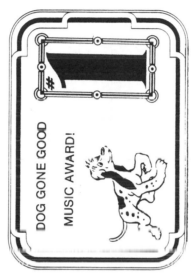

DOG GONE GOOD

MUSIC AWARD!

#1

WELCOME

_____ (name)

to

MUSIC CLASS

Congratulations!

creative drawing

MUSIC AWARD

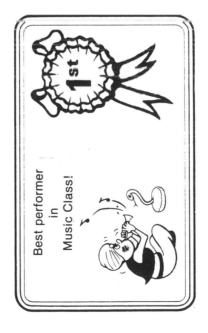

1st

Best performer
in
Music Class!

DON'T FORGET!

MUSIC

MUSIC SHARE-A-GRAM

TO: _____ DATE _____
(Parent's Name)

FROM: _____ SCHOOL _____
(Classroom Music Teacher)

RE: _____ CLASS _____
(Student's Name)

To help you recognize your child's success in music class or any area that needs attention the following observation(s) has/have been made.

	Exceptional	Satisfactory	Unsatisfactory
Shows musical aptitude			
Shows creativity			
Shows talent			
Shows initiative			
Self-concept in music class			
Fairness in dealing with classmates			
Self-direction			
Care of instrument and equipment			
Reaction to constructive criticism			
Observes music class rules			
Starts and completes work on time			
Generally follows directions			

over for comments ►

- -

RETURN-A-GRAM

TO: _____ DATE _____
(Classroom Music Teacher)

FROM: _____ SCHOOL _____
(Parent's Name)

RE: _____ CLASS _____
(Student's Name)

Please write your comments or questions on the back and return. If you want to be called for a parent-teacher conference, indicate below.

STUDENT RECORD PROFILE CHART

_____ (Student's Name) _____ Class _____ Year _____

Select the appropriate data in parentheses for each category, i, ii, iii, and iv, and record the information in the chart below as shown in the example.

i.—Unit Number for *Music Curriculum Activities Library* (1, 2, 3, 4, 5, 6, 7)

ii.—Date (Day/Month)

iii.—Semester (1, 2, 3, 4) or Summer School: Session 1 (S1), Session 2 (S2)

iv.—Score: Select one of the three grading systems, a., b., or c., that applies to your school progress report and/or applies to the specific activity.

a.
(O) = Outstanding
(G) = Good
(S) = Satisfactory
(NI) = Needs Improvement
(U) = Unsatisfactory
(I) = Incomplete
(—) = Absent

b.
(A) = 93–100 [percentage score]
(B) = 85–92
(C) = 75–84
(D) = 70–74
(F) = 0–69
(I) = Incomplete
(—) = Absent

c.
(R/P):
R = Correct number of responses.
P = Possible correct number of responses.
(I) = Incomplete
(—) = Absent

i	ii
iii	iv

Student's Name ——————— Class ——— Year ———

MUSIC SELF-IMPROVEMENT CHART (for student use)

a. On the back of this chart write your goal(s) for music class at the beginning of each semester.
b. On a separate sheet record the date and each new music skill you have acquired during the semester.

c. MUSIC SHARE-A-GRAM (date sent to parent)

d. RETURN-A-GRAM (date returned to teacher)

e. MUSIC AWARD BADGES (date and type rec'd)

1.
2.
3.

f. SPECIAL MUSIC RECOGNITION (date and type rec'd)

1.
2.
3.

g. SPECIAL MUSIC EVENT ATTENDANCE RECORD (date and name of special performance, recital, rehearsal, concert, field trip, film, workshop, seminar, institute, etc.)

1.
2.
3.
4.

h. ABOVE AND BEYOND: Extra Credit Projects (date and name of book report, classroom performance, construction of hand-made instrument, report on special music performance on TV, etc.)

1.
2.
3.
4.

i. PROGRESS REPORT/REPORT CARD RECORD (semester and grade received)

1.
2.
3.
4.

j. MUSIC SIGN-OUT RECORD (name of instrument, music, book or equipment with sign-out date and due date)

1.
2.
3.
4.
5.
6.
7.
8.
9.
10.